Supporting Microcomputers

Second Edition

Thomas P. Cavaiani, Ph.D.
Boise State University

Jim Joy, A+ Certified Service Technician
IKON Education Services

Susan D. Lanier-Graham
Thot Information Services

an imprint of ART Press

Publishers	Arnie Kuenn
	Craig King
Acquisitions	Paul Zagnoni
Managing Editor	Jamie Tillman
Technical Editor	Phil Shanks
Copy Editors	Erich Cameron
	Roxanne Graham
	Gerald Mallonee
	Wendy Mann
Illustrator	Erica Rossi
Photographer	Mark Tillman
Technical Consultants	Jay Mann, M.A., MCSE, and
	A+ Certified Service Technician
	Dan Rossi

This text was created using Microsoft Word 97. The primary fonts used are Century Schoolbook and Century Gothic.

Academic Research & Technologies
2700 North Central, 9th Floor
Phoenix, Arizona 85004
602.266.8530 ♦ FAX 602.266.6404

ISBN 1-58176-044-2

Academic Research & Technologies
an **IKON** Company

Table of Contents

INTRODUCTION

Welcome!

Welcome to *A+ Certification: Supporting Microcomputers*. This book is used to help you learn the basics of supporting microcomputers in today's industry. In addition, this text is also part of a program to help you attain A+ Certification.

A+ Certification is recognized worldwide as a standard of competency in microcomputer support. Certification indicates that you have the level of understanding necessary to install, service, and support microcomputers and peripherals. Many companies consider certification of high value in evaluating potential employees.

To help you understand the material throughout the text, there is a series of icons that point out information to which you may want to pay close attention. The icons included are:

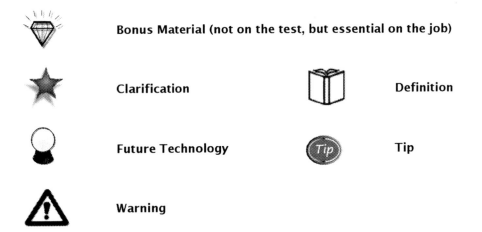

Bonus Material (not on the test, but essential on the job)

Clarification

Definition

Future Technology

Tip

Warning

Objectives

This text is designed to provide you with the information you need to maintain and service **personal computers (PCs)**. After studying the material in this text, you will be able to:

+ understand the basic hardware components of a PC

+ identify PC peripherals, including monitors, keyboards, pointing devices, scanners, modems, and cables

+ understand how to safely use common and specialized tools

+ understand and identify basic components on the motherboard

+ identify power requirements and troubleshoot power problems

+ identify and understand bus architectures

+ identify different types of memory

+ identify different types of microprocessors

+ identify various types of disk storage

+ understand the basic structure of a hard disk

+ understand how formatting is used to prepare a hard disk for storing data

+ use DOS utilities to maintain a hard disk

+ identify and understand various input/output devices

- identify different types of printers and understand how they function

- identify other hardware components, such as modems, cables, scanners, and multimedia hardware

- understand basic components of Local Area Networks (LANs)

- identify and correct common hardware problems and use software and hardware diagnostic tools

- respond properly to customer service question

LESSON 1: COMPUTER BASICS

This lesson presents the basic characteristics of personal computer systems using MS-DOS and Windows. After completing this lesson, you will be able to:

- recognize essential components of a PC system

- discuss the way computers process data

- understand basic computer terminology

Essential Computer Components

Although computers have changed civilization, they are only collections of electronic parts into which you feed data. The computer processes the data and provides you some specific information.

The following figure illustrates a typical computer system, although specific components vary.

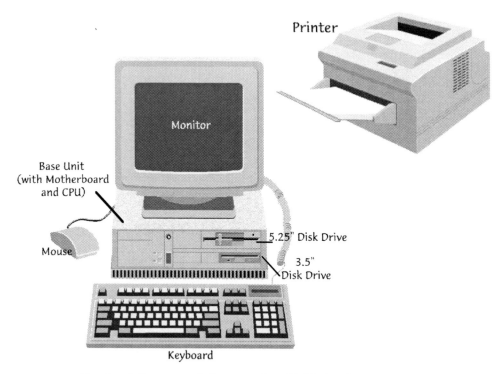

Typical Personal Computer (PC) System

A computer by many names ...

Many types of computers are in use today and each type has a particular function. The following list includes the common classifications of computers:

Supercomputers: huge, expensive (multimillion dollar range), lightning-fast machines used by only a few elite organizations.

Mainframes: large, expensive, centralized computers that usually contain massive amounts of data, such as a college database, bank records, personnel records, or mailing lists. Users connect to the mainframe through *dumb terminals*.

Minicomputers: systems of a size between mainframes and other computers.

Workstations: although this term is used often to refer to all desktop computers, workstations are traditionally high-end, fast computers designed for graphical work such as video production or drawing.

Microcomputers/Desktop Personal Computers (PCs): personal computers in homes, schools, and offices that sit on a single desktop. Although they may be connected to a network, they have a single processor inside.

Servers: powerful computers, smaller than minicomputers but with more storage and power than a desktop PC, used throughout computer networks. Servers usually store organizational data, files, and programs; control printers; and make resources available to all users throughout the organization.

Portables: computers you can take with you. Portables include laptops (10 to 15 lbs.), notebooks (8.5"x11" and 5 to 10 lbs.), subnotebooks (8.5"x6" and 2 to 5 lbs.), and palmtops and handheld PCs (fit in your hand and weigh less than 2 lbs.).

Input-Process-Output-Storage Cycle

The **central processing unit (CPU)** is the central control or brain of the computer and interprets and carries out every instruction.

All the processing in the computer turns raw data into useable information and is part of a cycle known as the **input-process-output-storage (IPOS)** cycle. This cycle includes everything that happens in a computer system. The following figure illustrates the process and explains how you can get the information you need from raw data fed into the computer.

Input—Use a keyboard to type instructions or enter data into the CPU, a mouse to select information from menus in Windows, or other devices such as pens, touch screens, or a microphone to enter data and instructions into the system.

Process—The central processing unit (CPU) acts on instructions stored in the computer's memory.

Storage—Because the computer has only temporary memory, long-term data storage occurs on some form of secondary storage. Secondary storage is typically a magnetic medium such as a floppy disk, hard disk, tape, or compact disc.

Output—Results of processing display on the monitor, are sent to a printer, or are broadcast as sound or video.

The cycle continues as you enter new information into the system or use existing, stored information. A **disk operating system (DOS)** manages every aspect of the IPOS cycle. Popular disk operating systems include Microsoft-DOS (MS-DOS), Microsoft Windows 3.x, Microsoft Windows 95, Microsoft Windows NT, and Macintosh. Each operating system contains a specific set of rules it uses to process data.

Processing Information

The heart of the IPOS cycle occurs in the **central processing unit**, or **CPU**. The CPU rests inside the computer case on a circuit board known as the **motherboard**. The following figure shows a motherboard with two Intel processors.

Motherboard with Components

The CPU is one of many **integrated circuits (ICs)** found in a typical computer. Each IC contains microscopic digital switches known as **transistors**. These transistors process all information you enter into a computer using a **binary** system, or **code**, of 0s and 1s. Each binary digit is known as a **bit**. The **American Standard Code for Information Interchange (ASCII)** specifies an 8-bit code for every

ASCII is a code that assigns an 8-bit combination of 1s and 0s to 256 characters, including letters, numbers, punctuation marks, and symbols. ASCII was developed in 1968 and is built into all PCs.

character and letter. For example, each letter in the word *Boise* consists of a specific set of 8 bits. The computer translates each set of 8 bits into a specific letter, much the same way you would translate the series of dots and dashes in Morse code into a specific letter. The following table shows the ASCII binary code for *Boise*:

B	01000010	This 8-bit pattern represents the letter B.
O	01001111	This 8-bit pattern represents the letter O.
I	01001001	This 8-bit pattern represents the letter I.
S	01010011	This 8-bit pattern represents the letter S.
E	01000101	This 8-bit pattern represents the letter E.

Each set of eight bits representing a letter in *Boise* is called a **byte**. A byte represents a single letter or character. For example, the word *Boise*, as indicated in the preceding table, consists of 5 bytes, or 40 bits. Memory capacity in the computer is measured in bytes, because the computer must process all information using binary code. The following table shows the way a single byte translates into larger blocks of characters.

1 byte	1 character of data
1 KB (kilobyte)	1000 bytes (actually 1,024 bytes)
1 MB (megabyte)	1 million bytes (actually 1,048,576 bytes)
1 GB (gigabyte)	1 billion bytes (actually 1,073,741,824 bytes)

The amazing part of computers' ability to process binary code and turn your raw data into useful information is that they continually compute these binary numbers at the rate of millions of calculations every second.

Throughout the remainder of this course, you will examine the individual components that make up the personal computer system, enabling the IPOS cycle to work.

Just how much is a byte?

1 byte (8 bits) = The letter S

100 bytes = A telegram

1 kilobyte (1000 bytes) = One half of a typewritten page

10 kilobytes = An encyclopedia page

100 kilobytes = A low-resolution photograph

1 megabyte (1 million bytes) = A 400-page book

5 megabytes = The complete works of Shakespeare

100 megabytes = 3 feet of shelved books

500 megabytes = A CD-ROM

1 gigabyte (1 billion bytes) = 1 pickup truck filled with paper

2 gigabytes = 60 feet of shelved books

20 gigabytes = A good collection of Beethoven's works

50 gigabytes = A floor of library books

1 terabyte (1 trillion bytes) = 50,000 trees worth of paper

2 terabytes = An academic research library

10 terabytes = Printed collection of the Library of Congress

Activity 1: Examining Basic Computer Components

Identify the components in the box the instructor provides. What are your initial reactions at this early point in the class?

What do you want to get from this class?

How do you foresee yourself using the information you gain in this class?

Review

A typical personal computer system consists of a **base unit** that contains the **motherboard** and the **central processing unit (CPU)**, a **monitor**, a **keyboard**, a **mouse**, and a **printer**.

A **disk operating system (DOS)** manages the computer's **input-process-output-storage cycle (IPOS)**. You can feed data to the computer (input) in various ways, including from the keyboard or by using a mouse. The CPU manipulates (processes) the data, and you receive the results (output) on a monitor or from a printer. You can save the information on a floppy disk or hard disk (storage) for use in future processing.

Computer storage is measured in **bytes**. Each byte consists of 8 **bits**, and usually represents a single character or letter. Each bit represents a 0 or 1, and every letter and character has a unique 8-bit binary code.

The **American Standard Code for Information Interchange (ASCII)** specifies the unique 8-bit code.

LESSON 2: TOOLS AND SAFETY

After completing this lesson, you will be able to:

- identify the tools used to work on microcomputers

- understand the safety hazards associated with troubleshooting electronic equipment

- recognize the impact of electrostatic discharge (ESD), electromagnetic interference (EMI), and radio frequency interference (RFI) on computer components

- use a multimeter to perform common troubleshooting procedures

Tools

When working on a microcomputer, it is important to use the appropriate tools. The following list includes the common tools as well as some specialized tools you can use to work on a PC.

Standard Tools

Tool kits for microcomputer installation and repair usually include the following items:

- **Screwdrivers** can be used to perform most microcomputer maintenance tasks, including removing cases, add-in boards, disk drives, and chips. Screwdrivers are available in many sizes and various styles, such as flathead, Phillips head, and Torx. Magnetized screwdrivers are convenient for picking up dropped screws, but they can accidentally magnetize floppy disk drive read-write heads. Use a screw starter or keep magnetized screwdrivers away from drive heads.

You use **Torx screwdrivers** to perform maintenance tasks. Macintosh and Compaq computers use Torx-type screws.

- A **nut driver** is similar to a screwdriver but has a hex-head socket end. You use a nut driver to reduce the risk of stripping screw heads.

- **Chip pullers** are tools specifically designed to pull chips from a circuit board with minimal bending of component leads or damage to the chip casing.

- **Tweezers** are convenient for handling jumpers and other small parts.

- A **part grabber** retrieves small parts and screws that you drop into the case. Loose parts accidentally left in the computer case can short out or damage the motherboard or drive electronics.

- **Needle-nosed pliers** help you remove jumpers and straighten bent pins.

- A **flashlight** lights the inside of the case. Even with good ambient lighting, you may find it difficult to see jumpers, labels, and connections inside the computer case clearly without a good flashlight.

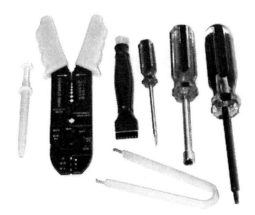

Tools for Servicing Microcomputers

Specialized Tools

The following specialized tools also can be useful when servicing microcomputers.

- An **offset screwdriver**, either bent or angled, helps you access hard-to-reach locations.

- A **multimeter** or **volt-ohm meter** enables you to test power supplies, cables, and terminators by measuring voltage, resistance, and current or amperage.

- **Extra batteries** are handy to replace existing CMOS batteries, which fail periodically.

- **ESD wrist straps** discharge static electricity from your body when you work on the internal circuits of a microcomputer. The wrist strap contains a 1-megohm resistor that protects you from an electrical shock of as much as 220 volts **alternating current (AC)**. You always should use ESD wrist straps when you service personal computers, but you should never use one when servicing monitors. The built-in resistor will not protect you from the high voltages present in monitors.

An **ohm** is a unit of electrical resistance between two points that produces a current of one ampere. One **megohm** is equal to one million ohms.

- Cans of **compressed air** clean dust from keyboards, cases, printers, or mouse devices. In a service department environment, a common shop vacuum set to *exhaust* is more economical and effective for cleaning PCs. Do not use compressed air or a vacuum for cleaning laser printers.

- An **AC circuit tester** helps you determine the correct wiring and grounding of wall outlets. You also can use a multimeter for this purpose.

- **Loopback plugs** let you test I/O ports such as serial and parallel ports. Many diagnostic software programs require that you install loopback plugs to completely test the port.

- **Gender changer plugs** convert male or female connectors to the opposite gender. Computer cables use opposite gender designs to help prevent improper connection to the wrong port. If you use a gender changer plug, be sure you connect the cable into the correct I/O port. Incorrect connections, such as plugging a serial printer into a parallel port, can damage the device and the port.

Software Tools

The following tools are useful when configuring hardware:

- A **startup, system,** or **bootable diskette** contains the DOS files necessary to boot, or start, a computer from the floppy disk drive. You use this disk to initially configure a system or if you have problems starting the computer from the hard disk. You should write-protect bootable and diagnostic software diskettes to prevent the spread of viruses by service technicians.

A **startup diskette**, or *system disk*, contains the programs necessary to *boot* a system, such as IO.SYS, MSDOS.SYS, and COMMAND.COM.

- **Diagnostic utilities** help you identify conflicts in your system and test hard disk drives, peripherals, and memory.

- **Data recovery software** helps you recover data that has been accidentally corrupted or lost due to a hard disk drive failure. The best data recovery method is always to create backup copies of data on floppy diskettes, magnetic tape, or other media such as ZIP drives. Also available are commercial data recovery services that may be able to recover information that DOS and third-party data recovery software cannot recover.

Be aware that using DOS or third-party data recovery software can corrupt lost data and make it impossible for the commercial services to recover the information. If the data is critical, go directly to a commercial data recovery service.

♦ **Anti-virus software** detects and removes viruses. You should scan computers for viruses before and after each service procedure, because problems can result from viruses. Technicians also can spread viruses with infected test and diagnostic diskettes.

You can take a few simple steps to avoid data loss due to viruses:

- install and use anti-virus software on every machine
- update the anti-virus software frequently; new viruses occur every day
- retain data backups
- keep a bootable diskette on hand
- scan systems at least once a week
- scan all floppy diskettes before using them

Safety

Though personal computers are generally safe in everyday use, they are pieces of electrical equipment that can cause electrical shock if you do not use safety precautions. To understand ways to ensure your own safety and that of those around you, you should first understand the sources of dangerous electricity in PCs.

Sources of Dangerous Electricity

In normal operation, computers and peripherals present little risk to users not working inside the computer. Although mild to moderate shock is more common, a user could get a fatal shock by touching the case if the electrical outlet is wired backward (reversed hot and neutral wires). Shock caused by faulty wiring is a serious problem. If you suspect faulty wiring, turn off the computer immediately and unplug it from the outlet. You can use a circuit tester or multimeter to confirm the problem, but you should refer the customer to an electrician if you discover faulty wiring. *Do not attempt to correct electrical wiring problems yourself unless you are a licensed electrician.*

The computer becomes more dangerous with the case removed, because contact with energized circuits is possible. Most power used inside the computer is low voltage **direct current (DC)**, making the technician more hazardous to the computer than the computer is to the technician. However, areas such as the power supply and the power supply switch do expose technicians to high voltages.

The PC power supply uses high voltage capacitors. If you open the power supply, you should first discharge any large capacitors.

 Repairing a computer power supply is rarely successful without specialized training, expensive test equipment, and manufacturer-specific schematics. Replacing a failed power supply is usually the best and most cost-effective option.

Power supplies with integral power switches have no exposed high voltage contact points. You can turn the power supply on and off if the motherboard is designed to comply with ATX specifications. The power button on an ATX-compliant PC is a low-voltage signal switch much like the turbo or reset buttons.

Power supply switches on towers and some desktop cases control the flow of high voltage AC power to the power supply. Even when you turn the switch off, dangerous voltages are present on the power switch contacts if the AC power cord is still plugged into the power supply.

Intel introduced the ATX motherboard specification in 1995. ATX architectures include built-in audio and video capabilities.

Monitors present the greatest electrical danger to PC service technicians. Even after you turn off and unplug a monitor, internal components continue to store thousands of volts and high current. Touching or getting close to high voltage components can result in a massive electrical shock that can be fatal. *Never wear a static grounding wristband or grounding system when servicing a monitor.* Monitors also present an explosion hazard. The **cathode ray tube (CRT)**, commonly called the picture tube, contains a strong vacuum. The CRT face is made of thick glass to protect the tube from accidental damage. The portion of the CRT inside the monitor case is not as rugged as the CRT face. If the rear surface, or yoke, of the CRT is cracked or broken, the internal vacuum will cause the tube to implode, or violently collapse, creating an explosion of glass shards and internal components.

You need specialized training, expensive test equipment, and access to manufacturer-specific schematics and parts to safely service monitors. It is unusual for PC service technicians to perform any service on monitors.

Preventing Electrical Shock

 An instant of distraction or carelessness can result in a deadly shock. Take a few precautions to prevent injury while servicing any type of electronic equipment.

Guidelines for avoiding electrical shock include the following precautions:

* **Never work alone.** A coworker may be able to provide emergency first aid, CPR, or to call emergency medical services.

* **Use only one hand** when working on electronic circuits. Technicians commonly put one hand in their pocket or hold one hand behind their backs while working on energized equipment. If you accidentally contact a high voltage current, the path to ground is less dangerous through an elbow, hip, or leg. If both hands are used, electrical current can pass across your chest and through your heart to find ground. Cardiac arrest is the most common cause of death in electrical shock accidents.

* **Wear insulated shoes.** Rubber soled shoes or tennis shoes provide good electrical insulation. Leather soled shoes or boots with metal nails in the heel or soles provide much less insulation.

* **Wear eye protection.** Wear safety glasses with side shields or safety goggles when servicing any equipment. Many companies require eye protection for all service technicians.

* **Avoid wearing contact lenses.** Service environments are frequently dusty, and the use of cleaning chemicals and solvents is common. Both conditions can irritate contact lenses. Normally innocuous solvent vapors can cause eye damage if trapped between a contact lens and the cornea of your eye. Many electronic

component manufacturers prohibit workers from wearing contact lenses in production areas.

- **Remove any jewelry** that could be exposed to circuits. Be careful to secure loose clothing, hair, and jewelry when working near moving parts, such as those found in printers.

- **Only perform service procedures for which you are properly trained**. Do not attempt to learn by trial and error. The cost of an error could be damaged equipment or a personal injury.

- **Discharge high voltage capacitors** and verify that they are discharged before working on power supplies or monitors. You must use specialized test equipment to safely discharge and test capacitors. *PC service technicians normally should not attempt to service monitors or power supplies.*

- **Do not work on electronic circuits when you are tired**. You must be wide-awake and careful to protect yourself and your equipment.

- **Never assume anything**. Always verify everything related to safety. Although a user or another technician may tell you that a PC's electricity is off or that the system is unplugged, you always should verify this yourself.

 A common effect of electrocution is heart failure. A working knowledge of cardiopulmonary resuscitation (CPR) could be a lifesaving skill for a technician on the job. The American Heart Association and Red Cross offer first aid and CPR training. Contact your local chapter for more information about training programs.

Electrostatic Discharge (ESD)

Electrostatic discharge (ESD) is static electricity transmitted from an outside source to a circuit. The human hand is the most common outside source of ESD.

Static electricity is a common and often useful form of electrical energy. Laser printers use static voltage in the electrophotographic (EP) process to transfer toner to paper, and manufacturers use it to evenly apply coatings to different products. However, static electricity also can have a destructive impact in the wrong environment.

Personal computer components are also susceptible to damage from electrostatic discharge. Static electricity discharged to the case, keyboard, or mouse of a computer can cause lockup or rebooting of the PC. In extreme situations, a computer user may have to wear a technician's static grounding strap or use a keyboard grounding strip to control static discharges. Most PCs are well protected from routine static electricity discharges. However, when a service technician opens a computer case, the system and all its components are susceptible to static electricity. You must take steps to protect existing and new computer components from ESD damage.

Sources of Static Electricity

Static electricity is generated by friction between two electrically dissimilar materials. For instance, a plastic material (synthetic clothes) rubbed against hair (human body) will quickly produce thousands of volts of static electricity. The painful zap you feel from touching a metal doorknob during the winter results from a discharge of 3,000 to 35,000 or more volts of static electricity. The human nervous system cannot feel discharges of less than 3,000 volts of static electricity, but discharges of less than 100 static volts can easily damage or destroy common electronic components.

It also is important to understand that electrostatic discharge can be caused just by coming close to a charged object. Styrofoam cups and silk ties are the leading offenders for proximity static discharges. *Keep work areas clear of static generating materials.* If you must wear a tie while servicing computers, be sure the tie does not touch components in the computer.

The following table shows the relative electrostatic properties of some common materials.

Electrostatic Properties of Common Materials

More Positive	Human Body
	Glass
	Mica
	Polyamide
	Wool
	Hair
	Silk
	Aluminum
	Paper
Neutral	Cotton
	Steel
	Wood
	Hard Rubber
	Polyester
	Polyethylene
	PVC
More Negative	PTFE (Teflon)

The following table shows the electrostatic voltage charges generated by common activities, as defined in the US Department of Defense Handbook, page 263, Tables II and III.

Typical Electrostatic Voltages Generated by Common Activities

Activity	10% RH	65% RH
Walking across a carpet	35,000 Volts	1,500 Volts
Walking across a vinyl floor	12,000 Volts	250 Volts
Working at a workbench	6,000 Volts	700 Volts
Plastic folder containing paper	7,000 Volts	600 Volts
Polybag lifted from a workbench	20,000 Volts	1,200 Volts
Worker sitting in a foam padded work chair	18,000 Volts	1,500 Volts

Effects of Static Discharge on Integrated Circuits

The integrated circuits in today's computers are susceptible to ESD damage. When an ungrounded technician discharges hundreds or thousands of volts of static electricity into a computer, the energy seeks the easiest path to ground. Frequently, the discharge path is through the microscopic circuits of a computer IC chip. Just as lightning can blow a hole in the top of a house or destroy a tree, static electricity can blow a microscopic hole through an IC. When the hole grows large enough to change the circuit's design characteristics, random errors begin occurring.

Symptoms of Static Damaged Circuits

More than 90 percent of all ESD damage does not immediately destroy circuits. Typically, a circuit begins to show symptoms of damage over time. It slowly changes its performance response, becomes intermittent, and then eventually fails. The ESD damage can take days, months, or years to produce a complete failure. This slow failure is called a **soft failure**. Soft failures cause intermittent error conditions and are the most difficult problem to troubleshoot and isolate.

If you suspect ESD is causing a soft failure, you can operate the PC continuously or at an elevated temperature to accelerate the normal failure process. Once a device fails completely, it is much easier to locate and replace.

Preventing ESD

Rather than isolating soft failures and repairing the damage, you should take the necessary steps to prevent the damage. The primary method of protecting computer devices from static electricity damage is to prevent the buildup of static charges. Several devices are designed for this, including the following:

➢ Using an ESD Grounding Strap

The **static grounding strap** is the most common anti-static tool that service technicians use. The strap consists of a conductive strap that you wear around your wrist, touching bare skin. A grounding wire attaches the strap to an electrical earth ground point. The strap dissipates in less than one second any static electricity generated when you move or walk. The grounding wire contains a 1-megohm resistor designed to protect you from fatal shock if you accidentally come in contact with currents greater than

220 volts AC. *Never wear a static grounding strap while servicing equipment that uses more than 220 volts.*

It is a common misunderstanding that holding a circuit board by the mounting bracket and avoiding touching any of the circuits allows you to handle a static-sensitive board without being grounded. The metal mounting bracket is usually connected to the electrical ground of the circuit board. Applying 10,000 volts of static electricity to the circuit ground will damage the circuit as quickly as touching a signal connection. In addition, it is usually impossible to touch just the edges of a board, due to the high density design of most circuit boards. The only safe way to handle a circuit board is always to ground yourself with a static grounding strap or equivalent device.

➤ Using Anti-Static Bags

Anti-static bags protect static-sensitive components and circuit boards when they are not installed in a computer. Although various types of anti-static bags exist, they all protect the enclosed parts from normal static charges. If you place a circuit board in an anti-static bag, you can handle it safely without grounding yourself.

The two basic types of anti-static bags are as follows:

▸ **Electrically conductive bags** are either translucent dark gray or dull black. The translucent dark gray bags are coated with a metallic layer that typically can dissipate 5,000 volts of static electricity in less than 50 microseconds. These shiny bags have an indefinite shelf life. The dull black bags are impregnated with carbon, which also quickly dissipates static electricity. These bags also have an indefinite shelf life.

▸ **Static dissipative bags** are usually pink, but also can appear blue, red, or clear. These bags, often called pink poly bags because of their color, are made of a transparent polyethylene plastic that has had a static dissipative chemical added to it during manufacturing. Dissipative bags can drop a 5,000-volt static charge in less than two seconds. However, the anti-static chemical does wear off after a while, at which point the bag no longer can protect static-sensitive devices. Manufacturers frequently use these bags for new parts and equipment.

➤ Setting Up an ESD Workstation

The ideal anti-static work environment for microcomputer service would include an anti-static surface workbench, multiple grounding points for the technician's anti-static wrist strap, and an anti-static grounded floor mat.

Working in a carefully controlled environment is not always possible for service technicians working at a client's site. When conducting onsite service, you should use the necessary procedures and tools to ensure a safe, anti-static work area despite the conditions.

To protect computer parts while working onsite, use the following guidelines:

▸ Leave static-sensitive components in protective packaging until needed.

▸ Connect the ground wire from your static grounding strap to a good electrical earth ground. Some static kits plug into a normal AC power socket to provide a convenient ground, but you should test the power socket first with a circuit tester or multimeter to ensure that it has the earth ground connected. Some three-pronged power sockets do not have the ground wire connected. If the PC is plugged into the AC power outlet and the system is turned off, the computer case is an earth ground. In this case, attaching the wrist strap ground wire to the bare metal of the computer power supply or case is usually a sufficient ground source.

▸ Do not place parts or circuit boards on any surface that is not anti-static. It is best to take the few extra seconds required to put circuit boards into an anti-static bag.

▸ Do not lay parts on either a bare or painted metal computer case. Though the bare metal of a grounded computer case will not have any static charge present, no resistance is present to slow the discharge of static voltages that might be present on the computer part. Slow discharge of static voltage is what protects components from ESD damage. The best practice is to place computer components in an anti-static bag immediately after you remove them from the computer.

Testing Static Grounding Systems

You also should check the equipment you use to control static electricity to ensure it is operating properly. Grounding mats should be clean, free from contamination, and undamaged. Check your wrist strap with an ohmmeter to verify that no connectors or wires are broken. You also can use an ohmmeter to test workbench and portable static grounding mats.

In more critical static control environments, you can use testing equipment that constantly monitors the condition of the static grounding system. Typically, an alarm sounds if static charges reach an unsafe level or if a grounding system operation fails completely or intermittently.

Electromagnetic Interference (EMI)

Any device that uses magnetic energy as part of its operation creates electromagnetic radiation. Strong electromagnetic fields can interfere with computer monitor operation and compromise data stored on magnetic media.

Sources of EMI

EMI comes from a variety of devices, including the following sources:

Electromagnetic interference (EMI) is interference caused by devices using magnetic energy, such as a computer monitor.

*   high energy power lines (220 or 440-volt AC power to a building)

*   large electric motors

*   pump or compressor motors that cycle on and off

*   florescent light transformers (ballasts)

*   audio speakers

*   CRT display devices such as televisions and computer monitors

Symptoms of EMI

The most common symptom of EMI in a computer system is a slow or fast wave that rolls down the monitor screen. If you can correct the strange display by moving the monitor to another location, the problem is probably electromagnetic interference. Strong EMI can cause unexplained corruption of magnetic data on floppy disk, Bernoulli boxes, or Zip drives. Backup tapes also are vulnerable to data corruption by magnetic fields. Extreme cases of EMI cause random computer lockups as well as badly distorted video display. Test equipment that costs about the same as a good multimeter is available to measure the strength of electromagnetic fields.

Controlling EMI

Shielding or relocating affected devices may control electromagnetic interference. You should look for any of the following problems:

♦ unshielded audio speakers

♦ AC to DC power converters used by PC peripherals and laptop computers

♦ high voltage power lines in or behind nearby walls

♦ two or more computer monitors placed close together

Moving the computer away from the source of interference usually corrects the problem.

Radio Frequency Interference (RFI)

Radio frequency interference (RFI) is noise in an integrated circuit that interferes with radio or television reception.

While ESD and EMI damage or degrade PC hardware and its operation, **radio frequency interference (RFI)** is caused by computers and affects other devices. Understanding RFI can help you troubleshoot and reduce or eliminate the interference.

Sources of RFI

Circuits in the personal computer operate in the megahertz (MHz) frequency range. This is the same frequency spectrum used by television and radio broadcasts. When computers emit radio frequencies, they can interfere with other nearby receivers. RFI typically causes television screens to display a snowy effect while the computer is operating.

FCC Certification Classes

The Federal Communications Commission (FCC) has established strict guidelines and regulations for radio frequency devices. Computers are in Class A and Class B categories.

FCC Class A certification regulations apply to any computer or peripheral equipment operating in an industrial or business environment. Class B certification applies to computers operating in a home environment. Because Class B devices usually operate in close proximity to other devices affected by RFI, the standard is much stricter. Manufacturers often release new computer designs with FCC Class A certification while working to attain the more difficult Class B certification.

Preventing RFI

Computers designed and certified to comply with FCC certification should not cause RFI problems under normal circumstances. If you do experience problems, you can try the following solutions:

- Move the computer away from the television or radio.

- Use a better antenna, coaxial antenna cable, or signal filters on the television or radio.

- Do not unnecessarily remove the blank plates that cover case expansion slots, I/O port knock outs, or drive covers.

- Do not damage conductive coatings sprayed on the inside of plastic case parts for RFI shielding.

♦ Add only FCC-certified circuit boards to computers.

 A computer owner is responsible for preventing interference with other devices. If computer interference disrupts someone else's television or radio reception, federal law requires that you turn off or remove the computer until you correct the problem.

Using a Multimeter

The **multimeter** is a multi-purpose test instrument used by electronics technicians. The multimeter serves a variety of purposes, including the following:

♦ the operation of circuits (the presence, absence, or amount of voltage)

♦ identifying wiring faults (continuity and resistance tests)

♦ checking for the proper wiring of electrical outlets (the voltage present between hot, neutral, and ground wires)

A modern multimeter combines an ohmmeter, an AC and DC voltmeter, and a current or ammeter. Meters that are more expensive may add special integrated circuit test settings, frequency counters, and capacitance meters.

It is critical that you read and understand the instruction manual that accompanies a multimeter. The manual will indicate the maximum voltage and current the meter should test. Voltage or current above the rated maximum values can damage the meter or present an electrocution hazard to the technician.

Ammeter

An **ammeter** measures current flow through a circuit, in amps. To function properly, the ammeter must be placed *in series* with the circuit you are testing, so that the current flows through the ammeter. Exceeding the rated maximum current level can damage or melt the ammeter. Use an ammeter to measure the charging current of a laptop computer to test the battery recharge circuit.

 You can compare electricity to water flow to demonstrate circuit testing. Water running through a pipe is like electrical current. To measure water in a pipe, you insert a water meter into the pipe (in series), causing all the water to flow through the meter.

Voltmeter

A **voltmeter** measures alternating current or direct current. You connect the voltmeter *in parallel* to the circuit you are testing. If you exceed the rated voltage of the voltmeter, you can damage or destroy the meter. To measure high voltages, you must have an optional high voltage probe. Attempting to measure high voltages with standard test meter probes can expose you to a fatal shock. Use a voltmeter to check the DC voltage produced by the computer's power supply.

 Using the same water flow illustration discussed with the ammeter, you can illustrate a voltmeter. The pressure of the water is similar to voltage. To test water pressure, you attach the meter to each side of the pipe wall.

Ohmmeter

An **ohmmeter** measures circuit resistance by injecting a DC voltage and measuring changes to the test voltage. You must always test the circuit for AC or DC voltage before using the ohmmeter. If voltage is present when you connect an ohmmeter, you will **damage or destroy** the tester. You must use the integrated circuit setting when working on computer circuit boards to avoid damaging the circuit. Use an ohmmeter to determine which wire runs from a motherboard connector to the case reset button.

 To continue the water flow analogy, resistance is like the friction of the water against the pipe. The longer the pipe, or the smaller the pipe, the more resistance.

Review

A variety of basic tools are used to install and repair microcomputers, including the following:

- screwdrivers (flathead, Phillips, and Torx)
- nut drivers
- chip pullers
- tweezers
- part grabbers
- needle-nosed pliers
- flashlights

Specialized tools used in the installation and repair of microcomputers include the following:

- offset screwdrivers
- multimeters
- ESD wrist straps
- compressed air
- AC circuit-wiring testers
- loopback plugs
- gender changer plugs

Systems tools you need when working with microcomputers include the following:

- a bootable DOS diskette
- diagnostic utilities
- data recovery software
- anti-virus software

Servicing computer equipment is generally safe if you follow common electrical safety procedures. Failure to observe these procedures can result in equipment damage and injury or death to service technicians.

Electrostatic discharge (ESD) is a stealth destroyer of computer equipment. Improper packaging and handling of computer components leads to ESD damage. You can follow simple ESD prevention procedures to prevent damage to parts, which can cause intermittent system failures.

Electromagnetic interference (EMI) and **radio frequency interference (RFI)** affect computers and other electronic equipment in the area. Understanding the difference between EMI and RFI makes correcting related problems easier.

A **multimeter** is a useful diagnostic tool. You must take common safety precautions to protect yourself, the equipment, and the multimeter from damage.

LESSON 3: INSIDE THE PC

After completing this lesson, you will be able to:

- understand the components of motherboards and associated performance issues

- identify power supply components, power problems, and protection from power problems

Motherboards and Components

The **motherboard** is the main PC circuit board, which contains all the
chips needed to make the system work. It also is called the **system
board** or **planar board**. The motherboard contains the following
components:

- central processing unit (CPU)

- optional math coprocessor on older systems

- battery

- bus controller and connector

- memory

- expansion slots

- power supply connectors

- keyboard connector

- basic input/output system (BIOS)

In 1995, Intel introduced new specifications for PC motherboard
architecture. This specification, known as **ATX**, contains built-in audio
and video capabilities and supports full-length boards for all sockets.
Non-ATX motherboards may have some slots blocked, preventing full-
length cards. The following figure illustrates a typical motherboard
configuration.

Processor   Battery   Expansion Slots

Cache Slot

Memory Slots

Floppy Disk Controller

Power Connector   Keyboard Connector

Basic Motherboard Configuration

This section examines the essential components on the motherboard.

Central Processing Unit (CPU)

All CPUs contain, at a minimum, the following components:

+ the **primary storage unit**, which stores data and instructions while the computer is processing

+ one or more **arithmetic/logic units (ALUs)**, which perform all calculations

+ a **control unit**, which supervises all activities of the CPU by *Cache controller* controlling the flow of data and instructions from RAM to the ALU

+ the **processor socket**, which is a grid of tiny holes that holds the CPU on the motherboard

- a **zero-insertion force (ZIF) socket**, which improves handling of the CPU by adding a lever in the socket to aid in removing or inserting the chip

- a **heat sink** or **fan**, which cools the CPU. Most 486 processors have a passive heat sink. Pentium systems require a CPU heat sink-fan combination or a passive heat sink cooled by its close proximity to the power supply fan

Bus

The motherboard also contains the **bus**, which is the pathway from the CPU to the adapter slots. You can visualize the bus as a highway connecting the various parts of the computer, enabling the system to transfer information between the various components. Every bus consists of groups of lines, and each line has a specific function.

- The **system bus** carries the control signals that direct activity on the bus.

- The **address bus** carries the memory locations, known as addresses, where your data is located.

- The **data bus** carries data between the CPU and the various peripheral devices, such as a printer or your monitor.

Basic Input/Output System (BIOS)

Complimentary metal-oxide semiconductor (CMOS) contains hardware data for a system, including the type of hard drive, amount of memory, disk drive information, and the location of the operating system.

The **basic input/output system**, or **BIOS**, is a set of instructions stored in a PC's read-only memory that starts each time a system starts. The BIOS gathers information about your computer, tests itself and the main processor chip, sets aside memory for itself, then reads data about the hardware from the CMOS. The BIOS serves the following three primary purposes:

1. initially configures system hardware when you turn on a system

2. locates the operating system and turns over control of the computer to the operating system

3. continues in the background as a type of interface between the user and the operating system

Input/Output (I/O) Addresses

I/O addresses are the paths that each circuit board uses to communicate with the processor. Every peripheral device on your PC must have a unique I/O address. I/O addresses are locations set aside in RAM, and all communication between the peripheral device and the processor are deposited in this RAM before the system distributes the messages to the correct locations.

The following table shows the I/O addresses of some common devices.

Device	I/O Address
COM1	3F8-3FF
COM2	2F8-2FF
LPT1	378-37F
LPT2	278-27F
XT controller	320-32F
Floppy controller	3F0-3F7
EGA/VGA	3C0-3CF
CGA	3D0-3DF
Monochrome	3B0-3BF

Common I/O Addresses

Direct Memory Access (DMA)

Direct memory access, or **DMA**, is memory that can be accessed without going through the processor. Often called a DMA channel, because it is essentially an open channel or pathway between the system and the memory, DMA usually transfers data between memory and peripherals such as disk drives.

Specific DMA channel assignments exist in every PC. Although they can differ, the common DMA assignments are shown in the following table:

DMA	Assignment
0	Unassigned
1	Usually unassigned, but can be the sound card
2	Diskette Drive Controller
3	Parallel Port
4	Cascade in Serial Input/Output
5	Usually unassigned, but could be sound or SCSI card
6	Unassigned
7	Unassigned

Common DMA Channel Assignments

Interrupt Request (IRQ) Levels

Interrupt requests, or **IRQs**, are signals from a device to the processor. When a device must access the processor, it sends an IRQ to the processor. The processor stops what it is doing and handles the request. Motherboards have IRQs 0 through 15, and every device must have a unique IRQ line to the CPU.

The following table shows typical IRQ assignments:

IRQ	Assignment
0	Timer
1	Keyboard
2	Secondary Interrupt Controller
3	Serial Port 2 (COM2)
4	Serial Port 1 (COM1)
5	LPT2 or Sound Card
6	Diskette Drive
7	Parallel Port (LPT1)
8	Real-time Clock
9	IRQ2 Redirected
10	Available (often a sound card)
11	PCI Bus or SCSI Interface
12	PS/2 Mouse
13	Math Coprocessor
14	Primary IDE (Hard Drive) Controller
15	Available or Secondary IDE Controller

IRQ Assignments

Performance Issues

CPU performance is measured by **clock speed** and **word size**. Clock speed is measured in **megahertz (MHz)**, or millions of cycles per second. Word size is the largest number of **bits** processed in one operation (16 or 32).

The CPU's performance is influenced by the following variables:

- **clock speed**, the number of clock cycles per second at which the CPU is capable of working. The two types of clock speed are both measured in MHz: **internal clock speed** refers to the rate at which the processor obtains information inside the CPU, and **external clock speed** is the rate at which the CPU communicates information to external components such as memory.

Complex instruction set computing (CISC) uses a processor designed so that each instruction can perform several low level operations such as memory access, arithmetic operations, and address calculations.

- **microcode**, the instruction set for the CPU, includes two microcode standards: **complex instruction set computing (CISC)** and **reduced instruction set computing (RISC)**

- **data path size**, the largest number of bits the bus can transport in one operation (8, 16, 32, or 64 bits).

- **internal cache memory**, high speed memory that is part of the CPU and holds frequently used information that the CPU needs. Using cache memory increases the CPU performance, making the entire system more efficient. L1 (level 1)

Reduced instruction set computing (RISC) uses a processor designed to rapidly execute a sequence of simple instructions rather than a large variety of complex instructions.

(Level 2)

- **external cache memory**, temporary L2 storage added to the motherboard. The external cache stores data during processing and can range in size from 64 KB to 1 MB.

Power Supplies

Every computer contains a **power supply**, which converts AC voltage from a wall outlet to the DC voltage needed by the computer. The power supply is the foundation of all that happens in a personal computer. A well designed and properly sized power supply can overcome many external power problems and provide stable power to hard drives and processors. Poorly designed or undersized power supplies can be the source of continuous problems.

The power supply sends a **power good signal** to the motherboard if everything is functioning properly. After receiving the signal, the PC starts up all components, and the power supply voltages rise to within their designated tolerances. This process usually takes only a few milliseconds after you turn on the power switch. If for any reason the computer experiences a momentary power loss that prevents the power supply from maintaining tolerance levels, the power good signal shuts down the computer.

The power supply provides the following DC voltages:

- +5 volts used by the motherboard and most circuits on peripheral cards. Wires that carry +5 volts are normally red.

- +12 volts used by disk drive motors and supplied to the ISA bus for use with an expansion card, if necessary. Wires that carry +12 volts are normally yellow.

- –5 and –12 volts are not used by most modern computer components. Most power supplies provide only very low current capacity for negative voltages. The wire that carries –5 volts is normally white. The wire that carries –12 volts is normally blue.

- +3.3 volts are needed by later models of Pentium-class processors. Older motherboard designs have a voltage regulator near the processor to convert +5 volts to +3.3 volts. Power supplies designed to the ATX standard provide +3.3 volts at pin 1 of the power connector.

Power Supply

A power supply provides four voltages, as shown in the following table:

Wire Color	Voltage	Proper Range	Current Range (amps)
Yellow	+12	+8.5 to +12.6	0.0 to 2.00
Blue	-12	-8.5 to -12.6	0.0 to 0.25
Red	+5	+2.4 to +5.2	2.3 to 7.00
White	-5	-4.5 to -5.4	0.0 to 0.30

Often, power supply failures can be at the root of PC problems. Some symptoms that point to power supply problems include:

Time/Date not working
Power on and system startup failures
Spontaneous rebooting
Periodic lockups under normal conditions
Intermittent memory errors
Hard drive and cooling fan cannot work simultaneously
Overheating
System resets
Electric shocks
Static discharges
Error messages 01x or 02x
Intermittent system failure
Printer and accessory failure
Intermittent fan operation
Flickering LEDs

During normal operation, a circuit constantly monitors each voltage output to ensure that it does not exceed maximum tolerances. Should a high voltage surge occur (usually because of a power supply regulator failure), the voltage monitor activates a crowbar circuit that blows the power supply fuse. Usually it is not enough to merely replace the blown power supply fuse. You must locate the underlying problem, which is most likely to be a faulty power supply.

Computer power supplies require a current load to operate. If you do not connect drives or a motherboard to the power supply, it will act dead.

Power supplies that meet ATX specifications also have power on and standby voltages that enable the power supply to shut down, or **sleep**. When the motherboard shuts down the power supply, the standby voltage supplies power to the motherboard's monitoring circuits. The motherboard is triggered by an event such as pressing a key on the keyboard, moving the mouse, or receiving a wake-up message. The motherboard responds by commanding the power supply to power up the system.

 Be sure to check the input voltage selection switch on your system. You must set the input voltage switch to the correct AC operating input voltage: either 110 or 220 volts. If you set the switch to 220 volts and plug the unit into 110 volts, the power supply will not function. If you set the switch to 110 volts and plug it into 220 volts, you will instantly destroy the power supply and possibly other system components.

The power supply also has a fan, which normally ventilates the computer case. Be careful not to block the intake or fan exhaust. If the power supply does not get enough air, the hard drives, processor, or other motherboard components can be damaged.

 You can purchase CPU fan failure and high temperature alarms from third parties to provide early warning that a serious failure is imminent.

Motherboard and Power Supply Connectors

Every power supply has a number of motherboard connectors. You must connect the wires correctly before the power supply can function properly. The three types of connectors are as follows:

- standard motherboard power connectors

- ATX power supply connectors

- drive power connectors

Standard Motherboard Power Connectors

When connecting standard motherboard power connectors to the motherboard power socket, you must keep the black ground wires together. If you connect the power supply plugs in reverse order, you will instantly destroy the motherboard when you attempt to power up the system.

The following table summarizes the standard motherboard power connectors.

Wire Number	Connector 1	Connector 2
1	Power Good	Ground
2	+5 volts	Ground
3	+12 volts	-5 volts
4	-12 volts	+5 volts
5	Ground	+5 volts
6	Ground	+5 volts

Standard Motherboard Power Connectors

ATX Power Supply Connectors

You can connect ATX power supply connectors only one way, which prevents the accidental reversal of connectors that was possible on older power supplies.

The following table identifies the standard ATX power supply connectors.

Wire Number	Signal
1	+3.3 volts
2	+3.3 volts
3	Ground
4	+5 volts
5	Ground
6	+5 volts
7	Ground
8	Power Good
9	+5 volts Standby
10	+12 volts
11	+3.3 volts
12	-12 volts
13	Ground
14	Power On
15	Ground
16	Ground
17	Ground
18	-5 volts
19	+5 volts
20	+5 volts

ATX Power Supply Connectors

Drive Power Connectors

Though the design of drive power connectors helps prevent incorrect connections, the use of Y cables to provide more drive connections is common. If you wire the cables backward, you will destroy the drive's electronics.

The following chart illustrates the standard drive power supply connectors.

Wire Number	Signal
1	+12 volts (Yellow)
2	Ground (Black)
3	Ground (Black
4	+5 volts (Red)

Drive Power Connectors

> ⚠ Be sure your power supply has enough power to support additional drives before adding any drives to a system.

Power Problems

Depending on your location, electric power from wall outlets can be erratic or unstable. The following are typical problems:

- An **overvoltage** is a higher than normal voltage. Overvoltages can be caused by lightning strikes, power grid switching, cycling pump or compressor motors, photocopiers, laser printers, or by many other common office equipment devices. A direct lightning strike can destroy everything connected to the power or telephone lines. PC power supplies can withstand a 10% increase in voltage without being damaged. The following are types of overvoltages:

  - A **spike** is a short overvoltage, measured in billionths of a second (nanoseconds) or millionths of a second (microseconds).

  - A **surge** is an overvoltage that lasts longer than a spike, measured in thousandths of a second (milliseconds).

- An **undervoltage** is a voltage that is lower than normal. Undervoltages are commonly caused by overloaded circuits. The following are types of undervoltages:

  - **Sags** are short periods of undervoltage.

  - **Brownouts** are prolonged periods of undervoltage.

  - **Blackouts** are complete losses of power.

Spikes, surges, sags, and brownouts often accompany the restoration of power following a total blackout. It is best to turn off all computer equipment during a blackout to protect it from unstable power when the electricity is restored.

Protection from Power Problems

Surge suppressors and backup power supplies can protect your computer from damage and loss of data due to power problems.

➤ Surge Suppressors

Due to their low cost, surge suppressors are the first line of defense against power problems. As a minimum measure, a good surge suppressor should be used to protect all computers. The following figure shows a typical surge suppressor.

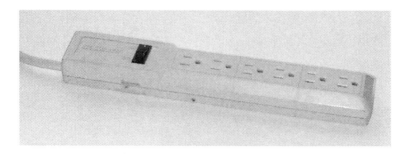

Surge Suppressor

You can judge the effectiveness of a surge suppressor in the following ways:

▸ **high joule rating**. A 200-joule unit gives your system basic protection. You can purchase surge suppressors rated as high as 1500 joules.

[handwritten note: Amount of Electricity in an amount of time]

▸ **let-through voltage**. This refers to the Underwriter Laboratories test (UL 1449), which certifies the design of a surge suppressor. 330 volts is the benchmark let-through voltage a surge suppressor can allow to gain the highest UL rating.

▸ **line noise filters**. Electrical signals of any frequency other than 60 cycles and signals too small to be considered a spike are called line noise. A television set that displays a snowy picture while a vacuum cleaner is being used is an example of line noise. If the surge suppressor does not remove line noise, the computer power supply voltage regulators do the job. However, making the power supply filter out line noise adds stress to the unit. Excessive line noise can shorten the life of a power supply or cause intermittent computer errors.

When confronted by a massive voltage spike such as a lightning strike, surge suppressors destroy themselves to stop the spike. Some surge suppressor manufacturers will pay to repair or replace computers that were protected by their surge suppressors, but still were damaged.

 Even the best surge suppressors cannot stop direct lightning strikes. Whenever possible, you should shut down and unplug computers from AC power during severe electrical storms.

A combination surge suppressor and line conditioner is one step better than regular units. While surge suppressors can stop high voltage spikes and noise, they cannot change or correct power that is a little low or high. Line conditioners, however, can adjust line voltage that is slightly off, regulating voltages from the high 80s to the 140s back to a steady 120 volts AC. Voltages outside this range cause the line conditioner to shut off power to the computer.

➢ Uninterruptible Power Supplies

An **uninterruptible power supply (UPS)** is the ultimate protection for computers. This backup power supply connects your computer directly to a battery. If the electricity fails, the computer continues to function with power supplied by the battery. The two major UPS versions are standby power supplies and online power supplies.

Uninterruptible Power Supply

‣ A **standby power supply** contains a battery and an AC power generator known as an **inverter**. A circuit constantly monitors the input AC power to ensure that it remains between the acceptable 100 volts and 140 volts AC. Some standby power supplies also have line conditioners to provide steady 120 volts AC. If the commercial power falls outside acceptable tolerances, the standby power supply switches on the internal AC inverter, synchronizes its signal with the failing commercial power, and switches the computer from commercial power to generated AC power, all within a span of two to four milliseconds. The computer continues to run uninterrupted until you exhaust the UPS's internal battery. Some UPS units also have an interface and control software that shuts down the operating system before the UPS runs out of battery power.

‣ **Online battery backup units** provide the same protection from power loss as standby units, but the computer always runs on the internal AC inverter. The online UPS receives commercial AC power and converts it to DC power. The DC power operates the internal AC inverter. If you lose commercial power, the UPS continues to use the DC power from its internal battery without any synchronizing or switching. Because the computer always runs on the UPS inverter, online battery backup units ensure that the 120-volt output is always steady. Online battery backup units with all the extras are the most reliable, but most expensive, form of protection.

Operating Your Power Supply

Both UPS styles rely on an internal lead acid battery for backup power. Lead acid batteries have the longest life span if always fully charged. Completely discharging this type of battery can damage it permanently. You should fully charge the battery in all new UPS units before you place them in service or test them. Testing a new UPS right out of the box is the best way to ruin the battery and void the warranty.

Lead acid batteries have a fixed shelf life that depends on how often you use the battery and how much it discharges before you shut it down. Under the best conditions, it is unusual for a battery to last more than two or three years.

 You should test an online battery backup unit every six months to ensure that it is still functioning and will work independently should you lose power.

To test a UPS, complete the following steps:

1. Plug the UPS into a power strip and plug the power strip into a commercial AC power outlet.

2. Plug a noncritical computer into the UPS to act as a load.

3. Turn off the power strip switch to simulate a power loss.

4. Allow the UPS to generate AC power for a couple of minutes before turning on the commercial power. A bad battery will usually fail within a minute.

 Do not unplug the online battery backup unit from commercial power to test it. Unplugging the UPS from the wall outlet removes the normal earth ground reference, and the unit may produce damaging voltage if it cannot measure its output in relation to ground.

The cost of surge suppressors is justified in almost every case. A good surge suppressor costs a fraction of even the least expensive computer, and a standby or online UPS protects high value computers. You always should protect file servers with a high quality UPS. Accounting, CAD, and software developer computers also may need UPS protection, depending on the cost of losing or corrupting data if you should unexpectedly lose power.

 Do not plug a surge suppressor into a UPS outlet. The noise filters in many surge suppressors will respond differently than a computer would to the UPS output voltage and can damage the UPS and the surge suppressor.

Activity 2: Disassembling and Reassembling PCs

To become familiar with the common components of a PC, perform the following activity:

1. Obtain an owner's manual for your PC and review its contents.

2. Turn on the power to your system. Observe how it starts; note which operating system boots. This should be Windows 95, Windows 3.11, or MS-DOS.

3. Shut down your system.

4. Look at the back of the computer. Use the owner's manual to help you identify all plugs on the back panel.

5. Remove all cables. Mark the plugs and both ends of each cable to help you reassemble the system.

6. Remove the cover from the computer and identify the following components:

    CPU
    ROM BIOS
    SIMM sockets
    hard disk drive
    floppy disk drive(s)
    power supply
    adapter cards
    slots

7. Remove the cables to the hard disk and floppy disk drives. Notice that the red line of the ribbon cable is connected to pin 1 on both the motherboard and the drive.

8. Disassemble the remaining components with your instructor's assistance. Remember to mark the connections to help you reassemble the PC.

9. Reassemble the PC. Turn it on to verify that it boots correctly. Correct any problems you encounter. Ask your instructor for assistance if necessary.

Review

The main PC circuit board is the **motherboard**, which contains the **CPU**, math coprocessor (on older systems), clock chip, memory chips, **ALU**, and **control unit**. The CPU is inserted into the processor socket. A **heat sink** or **fan** cools internal components.

CPU performance is measured by **clock speed** in megahertz (MHz) and by **word size**. The instruction set for the CPU is either **CISC** or **RISC**. The number of bits transported by the bus in one operation is known as the **data path size**.

The **power supply** converts AC voltage from a wall outlet to the DC voltage needed by the computer. The wires of different colors in the power supply provide different voltages.

Voltage problems include **overvoltages** (spikes or surges) and **undervoltages** (sags, brownouts, and blackouts). **Surge suppressors** and **backup power supplies** are used to protect computers from power problems.

LESSON 4: BUS ARCHITECTURE

This lesson examines the PC bus architecture and traces the evolution of PC bus structures. After completing this lesson, you will be able to:

- describe the way bus systems work

- discuss the evolution of bus structures used in PCs

Bus Systems

The bus is a system of pathways, embedded in the motherboard, that moves data from the CPU to the different devices attached to the motherboard. Some devices connect to the motherboard via adapter or expansion slots, where you plug in **expansion boards**. Examples of expansion boards include **video adapter cards**, modems, and sound cards. The following list explains PC bus architecture.

Industry Standard Architecture (ISA) XT AT

- introduced by IBM with the original IBM AT in 1984

- initially supported only five 8-bit slots; the ISA bus was later improved to support both 8-bit and 16-bit slots

The **Industry Standard Architecture (ISA)** standard allows you to add components by plugging cards into expansion slots.

- had extra pins on an additional connector to fit in a longer slot

- operated at 8 MHz

- supported **bus mastering**, or the ability to transfer data from one peripheral to another without intervention by the CPU or use of RAM

- allowed only one bus master board (1st H.77 MHZ)

Micro Channel Architecture (MCA)

- released in 1987 by IBM

- used in most models of IBM PS/2 and RS/6000 workstations

- operated at 10 MHz

- available in 16- and 32-bit versions

- supported bus mastering of as many as 16 bus masters

- allowed automated setup using the software program provided on a bootable reference disk. The reference disk software could program interface card settings to non-conflicting configurations: an early form of hardware plug and play.

The **Micro Channel Architecture (MCA)** standard is used in most IBM PS/2 computers. 16- and 32-bit versions of the MCA bus are available.

- limited third-party support kept the interface card prices high until IBM discontinued production of MCA

Extended Industry Standard Architecture (EISA)

- developed by PC manufacturers to compete with IBM's proprietary MCA bus

- supported new 32-bit interface cards in the same way the MCA bus did, but also was backward-compatible with the 16-bit ISA bus

- bus speed was limited to 8 MHz for backward compatibility

- had two rows of connectors: the top row of pins for ISA boards and the bottom row for EISA cards. The edge connector was twice as high and used a deeper slot

- supported bus mastering and allowed multiple bus masters

- used EISA configuration software similar to the MCA reference disk. Configuration software could control only EISA interface cards. The installer had to manually resolve possible conflicts between ISA cards and EISA cards.

Vendors Electronics Standards Association (VESA) local bus, or VL Bus

* introduced in 1992 as a video bus

* offered one or two 32-bit high speed connections

* included a high speed slot that could operate at the same speed as the processor, but only cards made specifically for the slot were compatible

* no software setup for the boards was included, as had been included in both the MCA and EISA buses

* no industry standards existed for this bus, and compatibility problems were constant

* the new PCI bus quickly replaced the VL Bus

Peripheral Component Interconnect (PCI) local bus

* designed by Intel for the Pentium processor

* introduced in 1992

* supports speeds as fast as 33 MHz 66   100

* supports as many as 10 PCI-compliant expansion cards in a single PC   3to4

* supports 32- and 64-bit implementations

* backward-compatible with ISA and EISA slots

- supports bus mastering and allows multiple bus masters

- supports software configuration of boards

- supports hardware plug and play

> Combining PCI and ISA cards in the same computer can lead to resource conflicts that you must resolve manually.

Personal Computer Memory Card Industry Association (PCMCIA) card bus

- released in 1990 and improved in 1995

- created by a group of Japanese manufacturers

- commonly known as the PC card

- used primarily in laptops, palmtops, and other portable computers

- created for memory but also used for modems and hard disks

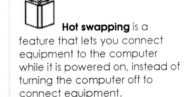

Hot swapping is a feature that lets you connect equipment to the computer while it is powered on, instead of turning the computer off to connect equipment.

- 16-bit interface originally; the 1995 version is a 32-bit interface

- hot-swappable and self-configuring (Card Identification Structure)

- originally did not support bus mastering; the 1995 version supports bus mastering

- bus speed, originally limited to 6 MHz, is now limited to 33 MHz

- available in three versions:

  - Type 1 (3.3 mm thick) for memory

- Type II (5 mm thick) for I/O devices such as LAN cards and modems

- Type III (10.5 mm thick) for hard disks

- thinner cards will plug into thicker sockets; for example, a type I card will plug into a type II or III socket

- provides performance similar to the PCI bus

- operates at 3.3 volts to conserve laptop battery power

(IntelProcessor mmx capabilities)

 Accelerated Graphics Port (AGP)

- dedicated, high speed video bus

- significantly increases the quality and speed of three-dimensional (3D) graphics

 Accelerated Graphics Port (AGP) provides a pathway, or bus, from the CPU to the main system RAM. AGP offers a 66 MHz, 64-bit pathway that increases to 133 MB per second for transfers, and burst mode provides up to 528 MB per second transfers.

- avoids competing for bandwidth on the increasingly busy PCI bus

- allows 528 MB per second of video throughput between the AGP video card and Pentium processor. By comparison, the PCI bus has a capacity of 132 MB per second data throughput to the Pentium processor, which is shared among all installed PCI devices (hard disk drive controllers, SCSI interfaces, network cards, etc).

- uses main system RAM to image textured bitmap 3D graphics, often requiring more than 20 MB of RAM. Pre-AGP video cards typically were available with 2 MB or 4 MB of RAM.

- AGP is only for Pentium II systems with the Intel 440LX chipset, but the new AGP-2 is for the workstation market

- AGP-2 provides a 500 MB per second typical transfer rate

 AGP-4, with 1 GB per second typical transfer rate, is due to be released in 1999.

Review

The **bus** is a system of pathways that connects the CPU to devices attached to the motherboard.

Some devices use **adapter cards**, or **expansion boards** that plug into slots on the motherboard, to connect to the motherboard. Video adapter cards, modems, and sound cards are examples of expansion boards.

LESSON 5: MEMORY OVERVIEW

In this lesson you will examine various types of computer memory. After completing this lesson, you will be able to:

* discuss system memory and how it is allocated

* identify types of memory used by operating systems

System Memory

The amount of memory installed in a PC differs from the amount of memory that is available to applications via the operating system. In theory, the amount of accessible memory is a function of the microprocessor design. In reality, PC designers must decide how much physical memory they want to include in the systems they market. The amount of memory you install in a PC is affected by several factors, including the following:

* the microprocessor installed

* the operating system (MS-DOS, Windows 3.x, or Windows 95)

* the cost of memory chips

Memory Addresses

Program instructions are stored at memory addresses in RAM. IBM-compatible PCs use the following four memory categories:

* conventional memory

* upper memory blocks (UMB)

* extended memory

* expanded memory

The following figure, a memory map of a typical MS-DOS-based PC, compares these types of memory:

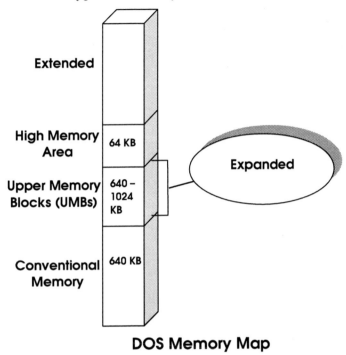

DOS Memory Map

Conventional Memory

Conventional memory today is the first 640 KB of memory available on a PC. The first PCs, however, were distributed with 64 KB of conventional memory. This figure rapidly increased as the price of memory chips decreased and software programs increased in size. By the time the first 286 computers were shipped, 640 KB of conventional memory was common.

Conventional memory is the first 640 KB of memory available on a PC. Conventional memory is the only RAM accessible to MS-DOS programs without the use of special techniques.

When you boot your PC, the operating system and any programs referenced in the computer's startup configuration files load into conventional memory. The remaining memory is available to other applications.

Upper Memory Blocks (UMBs)

The 384 KB area located immediately above conventional memory is called **upper memory blocks (UMBs)**. The upper memory area is intended for system use. Programs that normally reside in conventional memory, such as a mouse driver, also can reside in the upper memory area if space is available, freeing space in conventional memory for applications.

Windows 3.x and Windows 95 use UMBs to write to a disk or a network device.

Expanded Memory

The **page frame**, illustrated on the memory map above, is a section of memory set aside to shuttle the data between the memory areas. The page frame is actually *virtual memory*.

Expanded memory operates by swapping information in and out of conventional memory using a 64 KB **page frame** in the upper memory areas. The page frame, illustrated on the memory map preceding, is a section of memory set aside to shuttle data between memory areas. The page frame is virtual memory. **Virtual memory** is memory that appears larger to an application than it is, usually by using part of the hard disk as temporary data storage.

Expanded memory was a joint development project between Lotus, Intel, and Microsoft (LIM), designed originally to allow PCs to access large Lotus 1-2-3™ spreadsheets that would not work in the 640 KB of

conventional memory. Other
applications quickly took advantage of
the LIM expanded memory.

Expanded memory can be slow, due to
the extra time required to swap data
and programs between conventional
and expanded memory. This problem

Virtual memory is memory that
appears larger to an application
than it actually is, usually by
using part of the hard disk as
temporary memory storage.

was solved in Windows 3.x and Windows 95, when extended memory
(see following) was manufactured to emulate expanded memory.

High Memory

Originally, the Intel 8088 processor and MS-DOS could not use more
than 1 MB of RAM. When Intel designed the 80286 processor, they
broke the 1MB barrier, but the first 64 KB of memory over 1 MB was
unusable due to memory conflicts. Quarterdeck introduced memory
manager software to allow access to that lost high memory area.
Microsoft included a file, HIMEM.SYS, in MS-DOS versions 5.0 and
later that enabled portions of DOS to operate in the 64 KB high
memory area, freeing portions of conventional memory for other
programs.

Extended Memory

Extended memory, available only in 80386, 80486, and Pentium-
class processors (unless the user has special software), is the system
memory beyond 1 MB. Applications running in either a Windows or
OS/2 environment can automatically use extended memory. MS-DOS
applications can use extended memory only with the aid of additional
software.

Memory and Hardware Limitations

The design of the microprocessor determines the amount of memory a PC can access, or its **addressable memory**. The maximum amount of addressable memory on a PC is equal to two raised to the power equal to the address bus size. Therefore, an 8088 PC with a 20-bit address bus can address a maximum of 2^{20} bytes, or 1 MB of memory. The following table shows the memory limitations of the different types of processors.

Trade Name	Processor	Bus Size (in bits)	Addressable Memory
PC & XT	8088	20	1 MB
AT	80286	24	16 MB
386	80386	32	4 GB
486	80486	32	4 GB
Pentium	Pentium	32/36*	64 GB

*original Pentium was 32; later Pentiums are 36

Memory Limitations by Processor Type

ROM and RAM

Computer memory stores both instructions and data such as numbers or character strings. The system assigns an address to all data stored in memory so that the CPU can locate the data quickly. The three basic types of memory available to applications are ROM, RAM, and Video RAM. In this section, you will examine these types of memory.

Read-Only Memory (ROM)

Nonvolatile memory remains intact even in the event of a power loss or if you remove the memory from the circuit board.

Read-only memory, or **ROM**, is widely used to store software and data because it is **nonvolatile**. Personal computers use read-only memory to store the **power-on self test (POST)** and **basic input/output system (BIOS)** programs required to start the system. Accessing ROM is much slower

Check hardware

than accessing RAM; therefore, the system often copies the contents of ROM to RAM. This process is called **shadowing**. Though all types of read-only memory are commonly called ROM, there are four distinct designs of read-only memory circuits: ROM, PROM, EPROM, and EEPROM.

Basic input/output system (BIOS) is the resource management program stored on ROM chips. BIOS moves information from ROM into the main memory when you start a PC so that it is instantly available.

- **ROM** has data or software defined in the IC during the manufacturing process. Once produced, you cannot change the contents of ROM circuits. ROM is useful for mass-produced copies of the same program or data. ROM is a cost-effective way to distribute data or programs in large quantities if the information does not change often.

- **Programmable read-only memory (PROM)** contains no predefined data, but a programmer can add data using a hardware device called a PROM programmer. Once programmed, you cannot change the data. PROM is useful for smaller quantities of programs or data that might not justify the cost of producing a ROM.

- **Erasable programmable read-only memory (EPROM)** adds the ability to erase programmed circuits. After an EPROM programmer programs the circuit, exposure to intense ultraviolet light will erase the data. You can erase and reprogram EPROM a number of times. A characteristic feature of EPROM is a clear window above the IC that allows exposure to ultraviolet light. A paper label covers the window to prevent accidental light exposure. You must remove EPROM from the circuit board, place it in the EPROM eraser, and then place it in an EPROM programmer to change the data. Typically, you replace an existing EPROM with an updated program or data version and send the old IC back to the supplier for reprogramming. EPROM also is called reprogrammable read-only memory (RPROM).

- **Electrically erasable programmable read-only memory (EEPROM)** is memory you can erase and reprogram. Applying voltage to the erase pin of the IC erases EEPROMs, and you can load a new program or data without any special programmer or erasing equipment. You can perform the entire operation without removing the IC from the circuit board. Once loaded, data continues to be nonvolatile. EEPROMs have some definite drawbacks, however. They have less memory than RAM, and you can reprogram them only a set number of times before they wear out.

Random Access Memory (RAM)

Random access memory, or **RAM**, provides **volatile** read and write storage of data. Despite the names, both ROM and RAM allow random access to data.

Volatile memory is memory that disappears when the system is powered off, or if there is a power loss of at least 4 milliseconds.

RAM is available in two general designs: **static RAM (SRAM)** and **dynamic RAM (DRAM)**.

- **Static random access memory (SRAM)** chips have sets of four to six transistors. The complex nature of SRAM construction results in large, fast, but expensive chips with low capacity. Static RAM is used mostly in processor caches, where speed is important but size requirements are few.

Level 2 caching

- **Dynamic random access memory (DRAM)** chips have sets made up of a transistor and a capacitor. This simple design offers easier manufacturing, smaller size, and higher capacity than SRAM, but at a slower speed. Each set of a transistor and capacitor represents one data bit. The capacitor stores an electrical charge that represents a one or a zero for short periods. Each capacitor in DRAM chips must be refreshed periodically. If the memory capacitor is not refreshed within the required time, you will lose the stored data. Typically, the refresh rate of DRAM is 63 microseconds. This refresh rate is one of the limiting factors of DRAM. DRAM is used mostly for main system memory and on I/O cards such as video, hard disk drive controllers, and network adapter cards. In addition to the constant refresh rate, DRAM requires that both the row and column addresses be sent with each memory read or write. Access times range from 100 ns to 200 ns.

Conventional DRAM is obsolete and no longer used. The improvements include FPM, EDO, BEDO, SDRAM, and PDRAM.

▸ **Fast page mode (FPM) DRAM** has a slight performance advantage over conventional DRAM. FPM DRAM allows the row address to be sent only once if multiple columns on the row must be written to or read. Despite its name, FPM DRAM is the slowest memory technology currently available.

▸ **Extended data out (EDO) DRAM** improves performance slightly over FPM DRAM. By allowing the next read or write to start before the previous one finishes, a performance gain of three to five percent is realized. Due to this modest gain, EDO DRAM is prominent in some Pentium-class motherboard designs. However, EDO DRAM is not efficient at memory bus speeds faster than 66 MHz.

Pipeline burst is a common type of static RAM chip used for memory caches in which data is transferred all at one time without a break.

▸ **Burst extended data out (BEDO) DRAM** combines EDO technology with **pipeline burst** capabilities to improve performance over EDO DRAM. Though BEDO offers more improvement over EDO than EDO offered over FPM, most motherboard chip set manufacturers do not widely support BEDO, and it has never become popular.

A **nanosecond** is one billionth of a second. Nanoseconds are used to express the speeds at which electrical signals move through computer circuits.

‣ **Synchronous DRAM (SDRAM)** is a form of dynamic random access memory with vastly increased speeds due to the bursting technique it uses to predict the next memory location the system will access. Although SDRAM has access speeds of 8 **nanoseconds (ns)**, 10 ns, and 12 ns, the performance improvement is usually masked by existing chip set designs that use processor caching technology. Increased memory bus speeds of more than 100 MHz are better able to take advantage of SDRAM performance.

Design variations and the use of two different voltage levels make it confusing to select SDRAM. You must correctly identify the required specifications for SDRAM before installing it on your system. An incorrect match between the motherboard and the memory module can result in inoperability or damage to the motherboard and memory module.

‣ **RAMBus DRAM (RDRAM)** is a joint development venture between the Intel and RAMBus Corporations. When available, it will use an 8-bit memory bus and transfer data at 600 MB per second (as much as ten times faster than conventional DRAM). It will require modified motherboards, but will eliminate the need for memory caches. Commercial release is expected in 1999, with a later release of **next generation DRAM (nDRAM)** planned.

A new memory chip due to be released before the end of 1999 will store as much as 16 MB of information without a power supply. Ramtron, in a joint venture with Hitachi America Ltd. and Motorola, is working on **ferro-electric RAM (FRAM)**. FRAM works because of a ferro-electric film on the memory cells. Each ferro-electric crystal holds an atom that switches on and off like a DIP switch. FRAM chips will have the read/write capabilities of DRAM and SRAM, with the stability of ROM.

- **Video RAM** is used in video interface cards to build and display images. Video RAM receives new data from the processor and sends the current video image from RAM to the monitor at least 60 times per second. Several different RAM designs are available specifically for video card memory, including VRAM, WRAM, SGRAM, and MDRAM. In addition, FPM and EDO RAM are both used in some video cards.

  - **FPM** and **EDO** memory are used in low end video cards. Both of these are single-ported, meaning they only can send or receive data at one time. This causes slow performance when used on video cards. The low cost is the primary reason to choose FPM or EDO DRAM for video memory.

  - **Video RAM (VRAM)** was designed specifically to meet the performance challenges of video interfaces. VRAM is dual-ported, enabling it to send updates to the monitor while simultaneously receiving new information from the processor. VRAM is fast but expensive. High end video cards commonly use VRAM to achieve high performance and high resolutions.

  - **Window RAM (WRAM)** is an improvement over VRAM. WRAM is also dual-ported and can provide about 25 percent more bandwidth than VRAM by optimizing common graphical operations. Additionally, WRAM is easier to manufacture and is less expensive than VRAM. *Note: Window RAM has no connection with the Microsoft Windows operating system.*

  - **Synchronous graphics RAM (SGRAM)** is a single-ported memory design that operates at much higher speeds than FPM or EDO DRAM. It is optimized to cooperate with video acceleration features to improve overall video performance. This combination results in memory that is slightly more expensive than EDO DRAM but performs almost as fast as VRAM. Mid-range video cards use SGRAM, because performance is important, but the highest resolutions are not necessary.

▸ **Multibank DRAM (MDRAM)** is a significant departure from previous video memory designs. MDRAM divides video memory boundaries into 32 KB blocks. Previous video memory designs were configured in multiples of one megabyte (1 MB, 2 MB, 4 MB, and so on). If a video resolution required 2.25 MB of RAM, a standard video card would need 4 MB of installed video RAM.

However, MDRAM needs only 2.64 MB, or eight 32 KB banks, to view the same video display at the same resolution. Although MDRAM is single-ported, it supports **interleaved memory**, which provides almost the same speed performance as dual-ported RAM. Lower cost per bit and lower total required RAM make MDRAM an attractive competitor to VRAM and WRAM.

Interleaved memory organizes addresses in RAM so that adjacent locations are stored in different rows of chips. In this way, after accessing one byte, the processor can access additional bytes without waiting an entire memory cycle. Reducing this **wait state** speeds processing.

The amount of video memory installed on a system directly impacts the video quality. More video memory will provide sharper and more detailed images. The following list shows which display settings various amounts of memory will optimally support:

1 MB Video Memory
640 x 480, 24-bit color
800 x 600, 16-bit color
1024 x 768, 8-bit color

2 MB Video Memory
800 x 600, 24-bit color
1024 x 768, 16-bit color
1280 x 1024, 8-bit color

4 MB Video Memory
1024 x 768, 24-bit color
1280 x 1024, 16-bit color
1280 x 1024, 24-bit color

6 MB Video Memory
1600 x 1200, 24-bit color
1600 x 1280, 24-bit color

Controlling Memory Errors

Memory controls and handles errors many ways, depending on the type of RAM. The methods include non parity, parity, and error correcting code (ECC).

- **Non parity** assumes no memory errors will occur. Non parity is primarily a cost-saving feature used for RAM. Most other systems in a personal computer use parity error checking to ensure data integrity.

- **Parity** error checking uses a parity bit, or an extra bit added to each byte stored in RAM, to verify the accuracy of the bytes stored in memory. If the parity check discovers an error in RAM, the computer halts.

- **Error correction code (ECC)** memory is an emerging technology in PCs, although mainframes and minicomputers have used ECC memory for years. ECC memory can detect two-bit errors, correct the errors, and continue operating without interruption.

A company called Templex Technology is working on a new technology called **optical dynamic random access memory (ODRAM)**. ODRAM will combine the speed of conventional RAM with the storage capacity of magnetic media. A Templex technology called *temporally accessed spectral multiplexing (TASM)* would enable ODRAM chips to store as much as 8 GB of data per square inch. Rather than replacing conventional memory, Templex sees ODRAM as complementing it and foresees its use in mass storage devices, database buffers, and accelerators.

RAM Configurations

You can find RAM in three different configurations:

* **Dual in-line package (DIP)** is a chip with two rows of prongs. DIPs plug into sockets on the motherboard or an adapter card.

* **Single in-line memory modules (SIMMs)** have multiple chips soldered onto a single module, and the modules fit into sockets on the motherboard. Contacts on the front and back of SIMMs are electrically connected to provide some tolerance to connector contact problems.

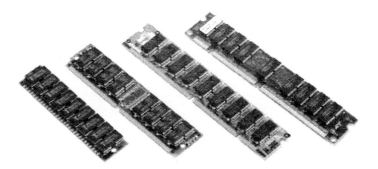

Single In-Line Memory Modules (SIMMs)

* **Dual in-line memory modules (DIMMs)** are larger than SIMMs and have electrically separate connections on the front and back of modules. This provides the additional communication lines required for higher density memory modules.

 Never clean any plated contact with an abrasive cleaner such as a pencil eraser. Any abrasive will remove the plating material and contact corrosion will occur, resulting in intermittent errors.

The manufacturing style of SIMMs and DIMMs helps prevent incorrect installation, because the two are mechanically unique. You must match the contact material used on the socket to the material used on the memory module. For example, if the socket has gold plating, the memory modules also must have gold plating. Dissimilar metals will cause bimetal corrosion over a period of time.

> A new technology, due to be released in 1999 from a cooperative venture by Hyundai Electronics, Mitsubishi, NEC, and Samsung, is called **synchronous link DRAM (SLDRAM)**. SLDRAM will have transfer speeds ranging between 400 MHz and 800 MHz. SLDRAM will offer more than fast speed, however. It will consume less power than existing DRAM and cost less than current high end RAMbus DRAM. SLDRAM is going to be marketed for notebooks, PCs, workstations, and servers.

The Memory Tree

Multiple variations of RAM and ROM can make it confusing to keep the relationships straight between the various types of memory. The following chart shows the relationships between the different types of memory.

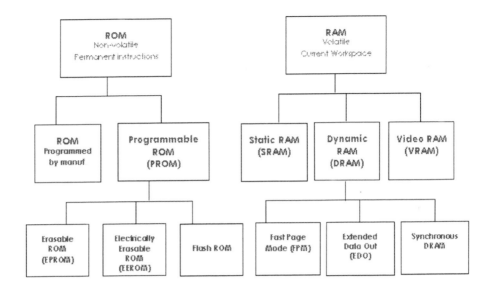

Activity 4: Investigating Memory

1. Start your PC. Exit Windows and display the DOS prompt if necessary.

2. Type **msd** at the command prompt to start the Microsoft Systems Diagnostics utility.

3. Type **m** to select the Memory option.

4. Close the Microsoft Systems Diagnostics window by pressing **Esc**.

5. Press **Alt+U** to display the Utility menu. Investigate both the Memory Browser and Memory Block Display options.

6. Use the menu options discussed in step 5 to determine the beginning addresses of the following:

    HIMEM.SYS _____

    ROM BIOS   _____

    Video BIOS _____

Review

The microprocessor design determines memory access, including the **address bus size** and **addressable memory**. The motherboard design, the microprocessor, and the operating system determine the maximum system memory that a computer can use.

Conventional memory is located at addresses 0 to 640 KB. **Upper memory blocks (UMBs)** occupy the area above 640 KB and below 1024 KB. **Expanded memory** uses a **page frame** in the UMBs to swap data and programs from conventional to expanded memory. **Virtual Memory** is memory that appears larger than it really is, because it uses the hard drive for temporary data storage. **Extended memory** uses addresses above 1024 KB (1 MB). The first 64 KB of extended memory is the high memory area.

RAM is the primary storage for the microcomputer, but this storage is temporary. RAM chips can be either **DRAM** or **SRAM**. RAM chips are available in **DIP**, **SIMM**, or **DIMM** layouts.

ROM holds permanent instructions; **PROM**, **EPROM**, and **EEPROM** are programmable ROMs.

Video RAM refers to the memory chips on a video adapter card.

LESSON 6: MICROPROCESSORS

Microprocessors are the brains of any compruter. In this lesson, you will learn about the chips that revolutionized the twentieth century. After completing this lesson, you will be able to:

- understand the evolution of the microprocessor

- discuss the performance of microprocessors

Intel and Motorola Microprocessors

Microprocessor chips have made astronomical leaps in recent years, both in speed and design. The evolution of the chip demonstrates the increased technology available as well as the vast differences in PCs over the past ten years. This section examines the history and performance of microprocessor chips, including Intel, Motorola, and PowerPC processors.

Intel Chips

Intel is the corporation responsible for much of the development of microprocessors during the past two decades. Beginning in 1971 with the 4004 chip, which powered desktop calculators, Intel has seriously impacted on the microprocessor industry. This section lists the features of the 4004, 8080, 8086, 8088, 80286, 80386, 80486, 80486DX2, 80486DX4, and Pentium chips produced by Intel.

A **DIP** or **dual in-line package** is the casing that houses some microprocessor chips. The electronic circuits are etched on a silicon wafer and enclosed in a rectangular plastic or ceramic case. This is all connected to pins lining both sides of the case. The pins fit on the circuit board.

4004

* introduced in 1971
* 2,300 transistors
* used in calculators
* 4-bit word size and data path size

Keep in mind that a **data bus**, or the **data path size**, is the amount of data the bus can transfer at one time. The **word size** is the amount of data the microprocessor processes internally at one time.

8080

* introduced in 1974
* used in the Altair, the first PC, and traffic signal controllers
* 6,000 transistors
* 8-bit word size and data bus

8086

* introduced in June 1978, used in IBM PCs and XTs
* 29,000 transistors
* 16-bit word size and data bus

8088

* introduced in 1979, used in IBM PCs and XTs
* 29,000 transistors
* a rectangular chip with two rows of 20 pins, known as a 40-pin DIP
* 5 MHz or slower (4.77 MHz in IBM's PC); turbo version: 8 MHz

Pin grid array (PGA) was introduced with the 80286 processor. Rather than the rectangular DIP used in the 8088 processor, the PGA was a square casing with pins protruding from the bottom rather than from the edges, as was the case in the DIP. This was the preferred packaging for chips with a large number of pins.

- identical to the 8086, except that the 8088 worked internally on 16-bit words but transferred them 8 bits at a time

- 20-bit address bus

- 1 MB addressable RAM

80286

- introduced in 1982 and included in IBM ATs beginning in 1984

- 134,000 transistors

- square 68-pin grid array (PGA)

- speeds from 12 MHz to 20 MHz

- 16-bit word size and data bus

- 16 MB of addressable RAM

- introduced protected mode

- ran at speeds three to six times faster than 8086/8088 processors

- operated in two modes: real mode, compatible with 8086 and supported MS-DOS, and protected mode, which enabled the CPU to access 16 MB of memory

- a **floating-point coprocessor**, or a coprocessor designed to perform advanced arithmetic functions, was available for the 80286. Designated 80287, it was available in 6 MHz and 12 MHz

Address bus 24 bits $2^{24} =$

Microprocessor with Pin Grid Array (PGA)

80386 (DX and SX versions)

- introduced in 1985
- 275,000 transistors
- square 132-pin PGA package
- speeds from 16 MHz to 40 MHz
- DX had a 32-bit word size and data bus
- SX had a 32-bit word size, but a 16-bit data bus
- 4 gigabytes (GB) of addressable RAM in protected mode
- supported multitasking for DOS programs

80486 (i486DX)

- introduced in 1989
- 1.6 million transistors
- 168-pin PGA package *very unstable*
- speeds from 25 MHz to 50 MHz

- original 80486 combined three chips: 386 chip, 386 cache controller chip, and 387 math coprocessor

- true 80486 had a 32-bit word size and data bus, a memory controller, and an 8 KB cache

  Level 1 cache

- in 1991, Intel introduced the i486SX, on which the math coprocessor was disabled

- 4 GB of addressable RAM

80486DX2 (i486DX2)

- introduced in 1992 as an upgrade to the i486DX processors

- speeds from 50 MHz to 80 MHz

- **clock doubler** processed data and instructions at twice the clock speed

- data transfer at clock speed

80486DX4 (i486DX4)

- introduced in 1994

- speeds from 75 MHz to 120 MHz

- used **clock tripler** technology (code named *Blue Lightning*) developed by IBM, which enabled the processor to operate at speeds approximately three times the clock speed

Pentium

- introduced in 1993

- 3.3 million transistors

- 273-pin PGA or 296-pin **staggered pin grid array (SPGA)** package

- speeds from 60 to 200 MHz

- 64-bit data bus and 32-bit address bus

- runs at 185° F; needs fan for cooling

- high speeds require special motherboard and bus

- includes two 8 KB caches: one for data and one for programs

- uses **superscalar processing** on boards with two processors, meaning that the second chip takes over if the first chip fails and that it processes two sets of instructions simultaneously (parallel processing)

- various speeds for desktop PCs, notebook computers, high performance desktop PCs, and servers

- includes **System Management Mode (SMM)**, which enables the processor to slow or halt selected system components when the system is idle to save power

- 4 GB of addressable RAM

Pentium Pro

- introduced in 1995

- 5.5 million transistors

- 387-pin SPGA package

- speeds from 150 MHz to 200 MHz

- 64-bit word size; 32-bit data bus; 36-bit address bus

- optimized for 32-bit applications running on 32-bit operating systems

- scaleable up to four processors

- L2 internal cache from 256 KB to 1 MB, depending on model

- **Dynamic Execution** technology adds to parallel processing. If information from the cache is not available when the processor is ready to process an instruction, the original Pentium has to wait. The Pentium Pro, however, uses Dynamic Execution to process instructions that follow the unavailable information while waiting. This speculative execution of instructions improves the efficiency of processor operation by about 33 percent

- bus width of 64 bits front side; 64 bits to L2 cache

Add 57 new instruction chip for multimedia technology

Pentium with MMX Technology

- introduced in 1997

- 4.5 million transistors

- 64-bit data bus; 32-bit address bus

- used in high performance desktop PCs and servers

> Intel is developing a 400 MHz Pentium II processor that works with a 100 MHz bus. Digital Equipment's Alpha chip will cruise at more than 600 MHz. Intel's first 64-bit processor is due to be released in 1999.

Pentium II

- introduced in 1997

- 7.5 million transistors

- uses 242-pin, **Single Edge Contact (SEC)**, Intel patented proprietary cartridge. Socket 1 is for processors from 233 MHz to 300 MHz and supports bus speeds as fast as 66 MHz. Socket 2 is for processors from 333 MHz to 400+ MHz and supports 100 MHz system bus speed.

- speeds from 233 MHz to 333 MHz and beyond

- combines the features of the Pentium Pro and MMX technologies

- 512 KB L2 Cache

- scaleable up to two processors

- optimized for 32-bit and multimedia applications running on 32-bit operating systems

- 64-bit word size; 32-bit data bus; 36-bit address bus

- 64 GB addressable RAM

- 64-bit system bus with Error Correction Code (ECC); 64-bit cache bus with ECC.

- used for high-end desktop systems, workstations, servers, and Web servers

You can upgrade an existing processor to an MMX chip using an *OverDrive* chip. However, upgrading is not as simple as it sounds. Two sets of guidelines should be followed:

To upgrade a PC running a 75 MHz, 90 MHz, or 100 MHz Pentium processor, you can install Intel's MMX OverDrive processor, but you also may need to upgrade your ROM BIOS. A utility is included with the MMX OverDrive processor to help you analyze systems for the BIOS upgrade, or you can download the utility from Intel at http:\\www.intel.com/OverDrive/ bios/index.htm. If you discover that you must upgrade the BIOS, contact the system manufacturer for upgrade information.

To upgrade a PC with a 133 MHz or faster Pentium processor or a Pentium Pro chip, you cannot use the OverDrive processor. However, you may be able to remove the existing chip and replace it with a new one. If you decide to do this, refer to the BIOS compatibility issue described in the preceding paragraph and verify hardware compatibility as well. A common problem is the dual voltage of the MMX chip. The MMX chip uses 3.3 volts externally and 2.8 volts internally. Many Pentium and Pentium Pro sockets cannot accommodate these dual voltage requirements.

Overdrive Processors from Intel and Kingston

 The availability of so many processors makes it difficult to decide which processor is best for specific applications. Although there is no fast rule, the following guidelines can be useful:

Pentium: choose this processor for daily business tasks such as word processing, spreadsheets, and simple databases.

Pentium Pro: this processor is an improvement over the Pentium for number-intensive applications such as complex databases and spreadsheets. This processor also is a good choice for a network server in most business applications.

Pentium with MMX technology: this processor was designed to run multimedia applications including games, full-motion video, 3D drawing, photo editing, audio/visual editing, and teleconferencing.

Pentium II: this processor was designed for desktop PCs, workstations, and servers used for business applications. This newest chip in the Intel family combines MMX technology with the number-handling capabilities of the Pentium Pro.

Motorola Chips

This section lists the features of Motorola chips used in Macintosh computers.

68000

- introduced in 1979
- 32-bit word size; 16-bit data bus

68010

- updated in 1982
- 68000 with virtual memory support

68020

- introduced in 1984 in Macintosh II and minicomputers
- capable of addressing 4 GB of RAM
- floating point processing

68030

- introduced in 1987 in Macintosh II
- increased speed
- 68020 with demand-page memory management

68040

- introduced in 1989
- Motorola's version of Intel 80486

PowerPC

- joint venture of IBM, Motorola, and Apple; used in Apple PowerMac, IBM RS6000, and Motorola workstations
- RISC microcode

Review

Intel microprocessor chips include the 8088, 80286, 80386, 80486, 80486DX2, 80486DX4, and Pentium.

System Management Mode (SMM) allows a system to slow or halt selected system components when the system is idle in order to save power.

The Pentium Pro microprocessor uses **Dynamic Execution** technology, which allows the system to process instructions that follow unavailable information while waiting. Dynamic Execution technology improves processor efficiency by about 33 percent.

Motorola processor chips include the 68000, 68010, 68020, 68030, 68040, and PowerPC.

LESSON 7: DISK STORAGE

Many microcomputer performance issues relate to memory or processor speed; however, disk storage capacity significantly impacts a computer's performance as well. Data is stored on hard or floppy disks. A typical microcomputer has as least one floppy disk drive and one hard disk drive. After completing this lesson, you will be able to:

- discuss the fundamentals of hard disk drives, including drive interfaces, performance, installation, partitioning, formatting, and the file allocation table (FAT)

- explain methods and tools used to optimize hard disk drive performance

- discuss the fundamentals of floppy disk drives, including media, types of drives, controllers, and cables

- understand removable media drives and tape backup drives

Hard Disk Drives

Hard disk drives, or hard drives, store data and programs permanently. Disk drive types differ in technology, interface, speed, and capacity.

Hard Disk Drive

Physical Description

Hard drives typically use two or more rigid aluminum or glass **platters** coated with material, in which data is magnetically recorded, stacked vertically on a shaft or spindle. The spindle connects to an electric motor that rotates the platters at speeds from 5,000 rpm to more than 10,000 rpm. A hard drive usually has two to eight platters and uses both sides of each platter.

If an older disk drive exhibits increased read-write errors, the drive heads might be out of alignment. It is possible in some instances to correct the alignment and salvage the drive.

As the platters spin, **read-write heads** read and write data to and from the platters. Each platter surface has one read-write head.

 Tip A **head crash** is damage to the head and platter caused by the read-write head coming into contact with the magnetic coating on the platter. Normally, the space between the head and the platter is only millionths of an inch wide. Damage to the read-write head or ferromagnetic surface of the platter results in irrecoverable data loss and can destroy the entire disk. New coating techniques protect both platters and the read-write head, allowing momentary contact without damage.

Each platter is divided into concentric circles called **tracks**. The tracks are divided into pie-shaped slices known as **sectors**. Each sector holds about 512 bytes of data. The tracks above and below each other on the platters are known as **cylinders**. The following figure shows a typical hard drive configuration:

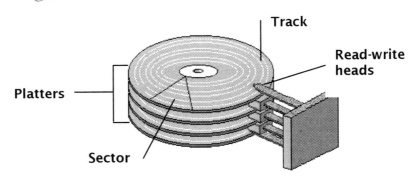

Hard Drive Configuration

Hard Disk Drive Interfaces

Hard disk drives require circuitry called **interfaces**. Typical hard drive interfaces include ST506, ESDI, IDE, and SCSI.

The following table shows the most common disk types and the number of sectors/tracks allowed on each.

Coding Schemes

Disk Type	Number of Sectors/Track
ST506 and MFM	17
ST506 and RLL	25 or 26
ESDI	34
IDE	Any number*
SCSI	Any number*

5m

Run Length

Real Level 2

* The maximum capacity of an IDE drive is 2 GB. EIDE uses logical block addressing (LBA) to break this 2 GB barrier.

ST506 Interface

An **interface** is a card or plug connecting hardware, such as a hard drive, to the computer so information can be shared between components.

The ST506 interface was originally used on the IBM PC. Two cables, the data cable and the control cable, connect the drive to a separate **controller**. The system transfers data **serially**, or one bit at a time, at rates of 0.625 to 1.2 MB per second.

Enhanced Small Device Interface (ESDI)

ESDI, produced in the early 1980s, translated and transferred data more efficiently than its predecessors. The ESDI interface uses RLL and has a transfer rate of 3 MB per second. It supports large drive capacities of more than 1 GB. When ESDI was introduced, it was used primarily in file servers and high end workstations because of the large drive support and faster data transfer rates.

A **controller** contains the circuitry required to run peripheral devices. A controller can be an IC located on the motherboard, or a plug-in expansion board.

ESDI has the same cabling as ST506, but uses different connectors. It uses a host controller that theoretically supports seven intelligent devices. However, in implementation, ESDI supports only two drives. Like ST506, it uses serial data transmission.

Integrated Device Electronics (IDE) 528mb

Integrated Device Electronics (IDE) also is called the **Advanced Technology Attachment (ATA)** interface. IDE was the first drive interface to include the controller on the drive housing, reducing interface costs and compatibility problems.

IDE drives transfer data in parallel and can support the **master drive** and the **slave drive** on the same cable.

In a master/slave drive arrangement, the **master drive** controls the **slave drive**. You can set drive jumpers on one of the drives to the *slave* position to disable the drive controller for that drive. When you reset the jumpers, the first drive controller takes over as the master to control both drives.

When you use two IDE drives on the same cable, you can access only one at a time for read or write operations. If the computer must read from the second drive while writing to the first drive, it must wait. In addition, every read or write operation involves the computer processor, which causes problems with multitasking operating systems such as Windows 95. IDE drives are best suited for single-user operating systems such as MS-DOS and Windows 3.x.

Secondary IDE controllers allow the operation of two additional IDE devices in the same computer. For best performance, one hard drive is attached to the primary controller and one hard drive installed on the secondary controller. In this configuration, access to both drives is possible without waiting on an operation in progress.

The IDE cable is officially limited to a length of 18 inches. With no protection from EMI, the flat ribbon cable can be a source of data corruption at faster data transfer rates. Newer ATA and industry standards incorporate better error detection and correction techniques to address this problem.

Ultra-ATA refers to EIDE adapters with the ATA-3 transfer protocol, developed jointly by Quantum and Intel. Ultra-ATA enables transfer rates of 33 MB per second.

Enhanced IDE (EIDE) is an industry marketing term that was coined by Western Digital. Most manufacturers use EIDE to refer to their drive enhancements; it indicates that the drive supports the ATA-2 standard. Other manufacturers that support the ATA-2 standard have called their drives Fast ATA and Fast ATA-2.

ANSI published the ATA-3 standard as a minor revision of ATA-2. It improves the reliability of high-speed data transfers.

Standard BIOS - only support 2 G of Drivespace

Small Computer System Interface (SCSI)

SCSI, an acronym for Small Computer System Interface, is defined by the ANSI X3T9.2 standard. The SCSI interface connects PCs to SCSI peripheral devices.

Small Computer System Interface (SCSI), pronounced *scuzzy*, is an independent data bus that functions without the direct intervention of the computer processor. Its command structure is more complex than previous drive types, allowing multiple read and write operations to occur concurrently. This makes it ideal for multitasking operating systems such as Windows 95.

SCSI provides clear performance gains when used in file servers and advanced multitasking operating systems, but operates at approximately the same speeds as other drive types with single-user operating systems such as MS-DOS. *8 devices on a chain*

SCSI was developed as a cooperative effort among Shugart Associates, NCR, and ANSI. The ANSI SCSI-1 standard was released in 1986 and defines commands, transfer modes, signal characteristics, and cable length. This initial standard supported an 8-bit parallel bus operating at 5 MB per second. You can connect as many as seven devices to the SCSI bus.

SCSI-2 was released in 1990 to address performance and compatibility problems. Three versions of the SCSI-2 interface were offered: Fast SCSI, Wide SCSI, and Fast/Wide SCSI.

You can use a SCSI-2 disk drive or host adapter with SCSI-1 equipment, but the equipment will run only at the SCSI-1 maximum speed.

- **Fast SCSI** has a 50-pin connector and transfers data 8 bits at a time, as fast as 10 MB per second.

- **Wide SCSI** transfers data 16 bits at a time, as fast as 20 MB per second. The connector has 68 pins, and the interface supports as many as 16 devices.

- **Fast/Wide SCSI** combines improved transfer rates with greater data width. Fast/Wide SCSI transfers data 16 bits at a time at speeds as fast as 20 MB per second. The Fast/Wide connector has 68 pins.

Currently, the SCSI-3 specifications defining the Ultra, Ultra Wide, and Serial interfaces are partially approved and should be completed in late 1998.

SCSI Bus Configuration

SCSI is an independent data bus consisting of one or more SCSI devices and a host adapter. The host adapter provides a connection to the computer data bus and arbitrates the operation of the SCSI bus. The bus also supports multiple SCSI host adapters.

Because the host adapter provides communication with all SCSI devices, the motherboard hard drive type should be set to *not installed*.

Termination involves installing electrical resistors, or terminators, at each end of a bus so that commands and data can travel uninterrupted along the bus. Correct termination prevents signal reflection at the ends of the bus, which can corrupt data.

Similar to other data bus designs, SCSI has specific requirements for termination and addressing, and you must adhere to the bus specification requirements during installation and configuration.

All data buses require electrical termination. The SCSI bus must have one termination at each end of the cable to avoid data errors, slow bus performance, and intermittent bus failures. Incorrect termination is the cause of most SCSI bus problems. You must terminate any device at the end of the SCSI bus and disable termination if the device is in the middle of the bus. The following figure illustrates bus termination of SCSI devices.

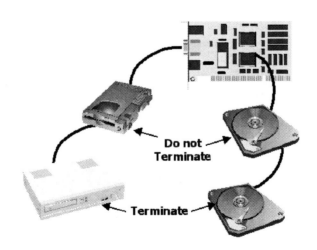

SCSI Termination

If you connect an external cable from the host adapter to an external device and terminate it, the bus will have three terminators. You must reconfigure the host adapter so that no terminators are in the middle of the bus.

SCSI supports the following three termination methods:

- **Passive Termination** is the oldest, simplest, and least reliable method. An array of resistors at each end of the cable provides termination. Additional resistance from the cable wire or connector contacts can change the total termination resistance enough to cause problems when you use faster bus speeds.

- **Active Termination** adds voltage regulation and resistors to provide termination that considers minor variations in bus resistance. Active termination is used with faster bus speeds.

- **Forced Perfect Termination (FPT)** adds clamping diodes to the voltage regulator and resistor configuration to maintain efficient termination. FPT almost eliminates signal reflections on the SCSI bus, and it is the preferred method of termination for SCSI-2 and 3 buses.

On all types of SCSI, active termination provides more reliable bus termination, and command queuing enables multiple simultaneous outstanding requests on the bus. Enhancing the SCSI command set added diagnostics, messages, and commands to support CD-ROM, scanners, and removable media.

The five basic methods of changing termination are as follows:

- Physically remove or install resistors in the sockets on internal SCSI devices.

- Change a termination switch on the hardware.

- Remove or install terminator plugs on external SCSI devices.

- Use the software setup program that was shipped with the bus or device.

- Do nothing if the documentation indicates that termination is automatic for the device.

 If you mix older 8-bit SCSI devices with newer 16-bit devices on the same bus, always ensure that the Wide SCSI is the last device on the bus. If an 8-bit SCSI device is on the end of the bus, only 8 of the 16 data lines can be properly terminated, and the Wide SCSI devices will have intermittent errors.

Try to avoid mixing 8-bit and 16-bit SCSI devices on the same bus.

Each device on a SCSI bus must have a unique address. When you install a device, you must manually set a unique address from 0 to 7 on an 8-bit bus, or 0 to 15 on a 16-bit bus. Although it usually does not matter which ID number you use as long as each one is unique, higher ID numbers do have a higher priority. SCSI devices communicate directly with each other, so device priority has almost no impact on performance. The SCSI device ID number priority order is 7, 6, 5, 4, 3, 2, 1, 0, 15, 14, 13, 12, 11, 10, 9, 8.

Duplicating SCSI ID numbers can produce unpredictable results or failures of the conflicting devices. Duplicate IDs will not, however, electrically damage the conflicting devices.

By default, the SCSI host adapter is 7, most hard drives are 0, and CD-ROM or tape drives are 2. Some host adapters, however, require that the boot hard drive be set to SCSI ID 0.

 Some new SCSI-3 devices dynamically assign ID numbers and automate termination to allow hot swapping of devices on the bus.

SCSI Signaling

The SCSI bus sends electrical data signals the following two ways:

*   **Single-ended SCSI**, the most common method, sends the data signal through one wire of the ribbon cable. Because ribbon cable has no immunity from EMI, data can be corrupted. To minimize interference problems, single-ended SCSI cables are limited to very short lengths that decrease as the bus speed increases.

*   **Differential SCSI** sends the data signal through two wires with one signal exactly opposite in polarity from the other. When the system receives the two signals, it compares them. Any interference mixed into the signal during transmission will have the same polarity on each wire. In this way, the system can easily detect and remove interference. Differential SCSI supports much longer cable lengths than single-ended SCSI.

Single-ended and differential SCSI signaling are incompatible. Connecting devices of each type to the same bus will result in instant electrical damage to both devices. However, you can convert both single-ended and differential devices by using adapters.

 Differential SCSI devices are more expensive and are used only when cable distance is a problem.

Hard Drive Performance

Performance is affected by the average access time, data transfer rate, and hardware and software caches. You can use various tools, described later in this lesson, to improve performance.

Average Access Time

* The **average access time,** or random access time, is the rating most frequently used to compare the speeds of hard drives.

* **Seek time** is the time required for the read-write head to move from one track (or cylinder) to another. Older drives had seek times as slow as 85 ms, but newer ones have times as fast as 5 ms.

* **Rotational latency** is the time required for the data to rotate under the read-write head.

Data Transfer Rate

The **data transfer rate** is the speed at which data moves between the hard disk and the CPU, expressed in megabytes per second (MB/s). The following table shows the data transfer rates of different drives.

Drive Interface	Data Transfer Rate in Megabytes per second (MB/s)
ST506	1
ESDI	3
IDE	3
EIDE	3-33
SCSI-1	5
SCSI-2	10
SCSI-2 WIDE	20
SCSI-3 (Ultra Wide SCSI)	40

Sector Interleaves (No longer used)

Interleaving data on the hard drive is used only with older computers, because interleaving data slows the data transfer rate to match the computer's ability to accept it. For instance, when data is written to a hard drive by a slow computer, the drive head writes data to fill one sector. Because of the slow performance of the computer, the hard drive platter rotates past the next sector before another sector of information is ready to be written. Without interleaving, the drive would have to rotate one full turn for each sector of data to be written. By skipping sectors so the drive head is over the correct sector when new data is received, synchronization between the drive and computer is optimal. 1:3 to 1:6 interleave ratios were common on XT computers. The use of drive caches, faster controllers, and faster computers has eliminated the need to interleave data on hard drives.

Caching

A **cache** is a memory area in which frequently used data is copied for quick access. When the processor refers to a memory address, the cache checks for the address first, before searching regular memory.

Hard disk performance is affected by the mechanical limits of its moving parts, but using a memory cache can enhance performance dramatically. The computer operating system, hard drive controller, and/or the hard drive itself may perform caching. The operating system uses system RAM to store recently accessed memory locations and can store data you send to the disks to increase apparent drive speed. The hard drive controller and hard drive also can cache information in additional RAM built into each device. Although SRAM or DRAM can be used on the hard drive controller, SRAM is typically used on the hard drive for read ahead and write caching.

Hard Drive Installation

The computer system BIOS includes drive parameter tables that list information about supported drives. The BIOS usually has a User Specified option for unsupported drives. The BIOS may have an Auto-Configuration utility that makes installation easier. Without this utility, you must specify all the parameters necessary to install the drive. You can reduce drive capacity if you install an IDE drive whose setup parameters do not exactly match the drive parameters. This is unavoidable in the following cases:

* ST506 interface hard drives require an exact match between drive parameters and a corresponding drive table entry in system BIOS. Mismatches prevent the operation of the hard drive.

* ESDI drives are always identified as drive type 1 (no matter what drive type 1 happens to be). The ESDI drive controller translates system requests to the correct hard drive parameters.

* SCSI host adapters exercise complete control over communications with SCSI devices. The motherboard drive type always is set to *not installed, drive type 0,* or *SCSI.*

CMOS - to set it to Not install +
drive type O

Hard Disk Partitions

A hard disk can be divided into areas called **partitions**. Prior to DOS 4.0, partitions could be no larger than 32 MB. DOS 6.2 supported partitions as large as 2 GB. Windows 95 introduced a 32-bit partition option (FAT 32) that supported partition sizes as large as 2 terabytes (TB). Windows NT supports a new file system, known as NTFS, which supports partition sizes as large as 16 exabytes.

The **primary partition**, or **active partition**, boots the system and is normally identified as drive C. The **extended partition** can be subdivided into different logical drives and uses drive letters D through Z.

Normally, hard drives contain only one partition. Multiple partitions allow you to install multiple operating systems on the same hard disk, to segregate directories onto different drives, or to use smaller cluster sizes.

Partitioning a hard disk will destroy data on the disk. You should back up all necessary files before partitioning. The FDISK command uses a series of onscreen menus to guide you through the process of partitioning a disk.

Hard Disk Formatting

Before you can use a hard disk, you must format it. Formatting prepares the disk by organizing the storage space in data compartments that the operating system can use to locate and retrieve data. The two types of formatting are high level formatting and low level formatting.

High Level Formatting

High level, or **logical**, formatting prepares each of the logical drives for data storage. In DOS and Windows 3.x, you use the **FORMAT** command to divide the tracks into more easily managed 512-byte sectors. DOS allocates space for files in units called **clusters**. Depending on the size of the disk, a cluster can contain from 4 to 64 sectors.

A formatted disk is divided into the following five areas:

- The **partition table** defines the way in which the hard disk is divided into logical drives.

- The **boot record** is located on the primary DOS partition and starts the system.

- The **file allocation table (FAT)** contains information about where files are located.

- The **directory** contains the filenames, sizes, and the last date and time the files were changed.

- The **data space** contains the actual data.

A high level format of the hard disk will rewrite the file allocation table, which effectively makes all data unusable. If possible, always back up data before starting a formatting operation.

Low Level Formatting

Low level, or **physical**, formatting physically prepares the disk by defining magnetic sector and track boundaries.

ST506 and ESDI interface hard disks require low level formatting when installed in a computer. The hard disk drive controller performs a low level format that is unique to that controller, and changing the controller manufacturer, or even changing to a different model controller by the same manufacturer, usually requires a new low level format to be performed on all installed hard disks.

Because controllers are already installed, or embedded, on IDE and SCSI hard disks, the drive manufacturer performs the low level format at the factory.

As hard disks age, the strength of magnetic data weakens. Every time the drive head passes over data, the magnetic strength of the data bit is weakened a little. High temperatures also weaken magnetic fields used to store data. Because sector and track magnetic data is written only during the low level format, it can eventually become too weak to read reliably. Low level formatting of older drives can correct this problem.

IDE hard disks have **servo** alignment tracks to improve locating closely spaced data. Older low level format programs will overwrite these alignment tracks. If the alignment track is lost, an IDE disk may function unreliably or not at all. Be sure to use diagnostic utilities that are certified for IDE disks if a low level format is needed.

As with partitioning and high level formatting, a low level format will destroy all data on the hard disk.

Master Boot Record (MBR)

When a computer starts, the BIOS program stored in ROM supplies enough information to direct the computer to look at the floppy disk drive or the hard disk drive for a master boot record. The **master boot record** contains a master partition table and master boot code. The master partition table contains descriptions of the hard disk partitions, and the master boot code contains enough information to locate and load the operating system. The master boot code always resides at head 0, cylinder 0, and sector 1 of the floppy or hard disk.

Because all computers require a master boot code, it is a favorite target of virus programmers.

The File Allocation Table

The **file allocation table (FAT)** contains information about where files are stored on the disk's data area. The FAT follows the boot record. Because of the critical nature of the FAT, two copies are stored on the disk.

The FAT records the location and availability of clusters on the hard disk drive. A file must occupy at least one cluster, regardless of the file size. Each FAT entry is connected to the next cluster by a **pointer**. An entire file consists of the chain of clusters.

 The **FORMAT** command erases the FAT, which contains the locations of all files and directories, but leaves data unchanged.

The three encoding methods for storing data on a hard drive are as follows:

*   **modified frequency modulation (MFM)**

*   **run length limited (RLL)**

*   **advanced run length limited (ARLL)**

Optimizing Hard Disk Drive Performance

Once the hard disk is formatted and programs are installed, you can use numerous on-going strategies to ensure that the disk performs at its best. These strategies include the following:

♦ mending file fragmentation

♦ deleting lost clusters

♦ optimizing available cluster size

♦ running SCANDISK

♦ using SMARTDrive (DOS systems only)

♦ using a RAM drive

File Fragmentation

To use hard disk space efficiently, disk operating systems allow file fragmentation, but fragmentation can lead to slow file access. A file can become fragmented when it has more data written to it. New data is written to the next available cluster, regardless of the location of that cluster on the disk. Eventually, parts or fragments of the file are scattered all over the disk. The DOS **DEFRAG** command is used to remove fragmentation. Windows 95 provides accessory programs that can defragment the hard disk on a scheduled basis.

Fragmentation is when parts of a single file are scattered to various locations on the disk.

Defragmentation utilities improve disk access time by moving clusters of files to contiguous locations. The defragmentation utility places unusual stress on the hard disk drive as it reads and moves fragments around the entire disk. It is safest to perform a full backup prior to starting a defragmentation operation.

Both DOS and Windows 95 include defragmentation utilities. The DOS DEFRAG command removes fragmentation in a DOS/Windows 3.x environment, and the **Defragmentation utility** in Windows 95 provides regularly scheduled maintenance and defragmentation of your hard disk.

 Do not use DOS DEFRAG when running Windows 3.x. Typing DEFRAG at a Windows DOS prompt generates the following warning:

Microsoft Defrag will not run in multitasking environments. Multitasking environments such as Windows maintain open files and may write to the disk. Because these disk writes are unpredictable, Microsoft Defrag will not run. You must switch to a single task environment to run Microsoft Defrag.

Keep in mind that this warning does not apply to Windows 95. Use the new Windows 95 defragmentation utility rather than the DEFRAG command.

Lost Clusters

Lost clusters indicate that the FAT thinks a cluster is in use but cannot link the cluster to a file. Normal files contain a starting directory entry followed by a list of linked clusters that represent all the clusters occupied by the file. Lost clusters have entries in the FAT but do not indicate a link back to a valid file cluster.

Lost clusters are fairly common and are usually caused by interrupted operations such as when a program freezes, the computer locks up, or power is lost unexpectedly. Windows 95 has a feature that automatically scans for drive errors when the system is not properly shut down.

 You should never turn off a computer without first exiting all programs.

The file system does not use disk space used by lost clusters, which wastes disk space. The DOS and NT **CHKDSK/F** command in DOS and Windows 3.x attaches a filename to each lost cluster to allow you to delete each one. It is generally not practical to recover data from lost clusters. Windows 95 and MS-DOS 6.x provide a more thorough utility called SCANDISK.

Cross-Linked Files

Cross-linked files are two different files in the FAT that claim the same cluster number as part of their file. Cross-linked files are not normal and indicate a much more serious problem than lost clusters. Diagnostic utilities will indicate both files that claim the same data cluster. When files are cross-linked, you can be certain that one of the files is already corrupt. You can try to determine which file correctly claims the cluster and salvage one of the two files in question, but often the only choice is to delete both files and restore both from a backup.

Invalid Files and Directories

If the file or directory structure is so corrupt that the operating system cannot identify it, the entry is classified as **invalid**. Sometimes disk diagnostics can repair this error. Multiple invalid files or directories may indicate a hard disk drive controller failure or soft head crash. A soft head crash damages a data area but does not destroy the read-write head.

ScanDisk

ScanDisk is a full-featured disk analysis and repair program included in both Windows 95 and MS-DOS 6.x. ScanDisk tests the file structure of your hard disk, including the file allocation table, for errors. It performs a surface scan of your disk to identify any areas that are failing. In many cases, ScanDisk can recover data from marginal areas. It is designed to work on both uncompressed drives and drives that were compressed using DriveSpace.

You run ScanDisk by typing **scandisk** at an MS-DOS prompt or by selecting the ScanDisk icon in Windows 95. If ScanDisk finds a problem, it displays a dialog box explaining the problem and requests confirmation to repair it. CHKDSK performs similar functions in Windows NT.

Hard Drive Power and Protection

Hard disk drives obtain their power from the PC's power supply. The power cable supplies +5 volts DC for logic circuit operation, +12 volts *(5+ volts)* DC for drive motor operation, and ground. The power connector is keyed to prevent incorrect connection.

If a Y power splitter is used to connect more drives than the power supply has connections for, be careful to verify the Y cable is correctly wired. A miswired Y cable (+5V and +12V reversed) will instantly destroy the drive when you turn on the power. Also, verify that the power supply has enough capacity to provide sufficient power to each device in the computer.

Hard drives today commonly include these advanced technology features:

Magneto-Resistive (MR) heads reduce the number of disk and heads necessary on a system.

Self-Monitoring Analysis and Reporting Technology (SMART) warns end users when hard drive failure is imminent.

PRML digital data channel capability increases media-to-buffer transfer rates.

Floppy Disk Drives

Floppy disk drives are slower and have much lower capacity than hard disk drives. Floppy disk drives typically are used to install application software, transport files, exchange data, and back up information. Components include the drive, diskettes, the controller, and the cables.

Floppy Disk Drive

Drives

Standard floppy disk drives support either double-density or high-density floppy disks. High-density disk drives support both densities, but you cannot use a high-density diskette in a double-density drive. MS-DOS and Windows reserve the letters *A* and *B* to designate multiple floppy disk drives. Data transfer rates are shown in the following table.

Drive Density	Data Transfer Rate
Double-density	250 kilobits per second (Kbps)
High-density	500 kilobits per second (Kbps)
Extra-high density	1 megabit per second (Mbps)

Data Transfer Rates by Drive Density

Diskettes

Density refers to how tightly the disk packs data. Though some double-density diskettes still exist, most in use today are high-density. Extra-high density 3.5" diskettes with a capacity of 2.88 MB also are available.

Floppy disk drives read data stored on disks, or diskettes. Storage capacity is measured in KB and MB and is determined by **density** and disk size.

The following table shows the most common disk configurations:

Size	Capacity	
	Double-Density	**High-Density**
5.25"	360 KB	1.2 MB
3.5"	720 KB	1.44 MB

Diskette Capacities

Controllers

Controllers translate digital data from the computer into an electronic format for the drive. The controller can be separate from or integrated into the motherboard.

The BIOS defines support for a 3.5" drive. Many BIOS automatic setup programs are able to detect the presence of a 5.25" or 3.5" floppy drive, but cannot distinguish between low or high density. If the system automatically detects the floppy disk drive but will not work properly, you should verify that the correct capacity is set in the system BIOS. Most microcomputers sold after 1989 support 3.5" drives.

If the disk drive has trouble reading several diskettes, the problem is likely to be dirt and dust built up on the drive's read-write heads. To clean a diskette:

- use compressed air to blow out loose dust
- use a diskette cleaning kit

Cables

Ribbon cables connect floppy disk drives to the controller. The cable
has a twist (reversing conductors 9 through 16), which electrically
identifies that the drive plugged into the end of the cable is the
primary drive, or drive A, and that the drive plugged into the middle of
the cable is the secondary drive, or drive B.

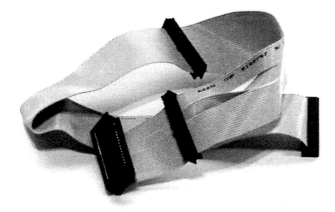

Ribbon Cable

 ST506 hard disk drives used the same size of cable with a
twist to identify multiple drives. The hard drive cable twist
is on the opposite side of the cable from the twist on a
floppy drive cable. The two cables are easily confused.
ST506 interface hard drives were very popular but are
rarely used now.

Other Types of Drives

External Drives

When the IBM PC was introduced, floppy disk drives and hard disk drives were too large to fit inside a computer case. External floppy disk and hard disk drives were options. With the development of floppy and hard drives that were 5.25" or smaller, drives could be mounted internally. External drives are used commonly with computers such as laptops that do not have enough room for internal drives. External drives also can be configured into **drive arrays** for high end computers or servers.

Drive Arrays

A **drive array** is a collection of multiple independent drives in one chassis or multiple drives that act as one logical drive. The expression "drive array" is a common way to refer to a RAID array.

In 1988, Professors Patterson, Gibson, and Katz of the University of California at Berkeley developed seven techniques called **redundant array of independent drives (RAID)** levels 0 through 6. Industry manufacturers produced commercial drive products and controllers using one or more combinations of the RAID level definitions. In 1992, the **RAID Advisory Board (RAB)** was formed to formalize the haphazard implementation of RAID products.

RAID was originally defined with seven levels:

Striping is a technique that spreads data over multiple disk drives. While disk striping can speed operations that retrieve data, it offers no disk failure protection. You can implement disk striping on single-user and multi-user systems, with the basic difference being the size of the striping unit.

- **RAID Level 0** uses **striping** across multiple drives to provide faster read and write operations. Because a failure of any one drive in a RAID 0 array results in the failure of the entire array, this is a **fault-intolerant** configuration. It is used where performance is needed but not failure protection.

1 HD 1mirror

Mirrored drives use a pair of drives to constantly keep a redundant copy of all data. Should one drive fail, the other continues operation without loss of data. Mirrored hard drives improve performance of read and write operations if connected using separate controllers.

- **RAID Level 1** uses preexisting techniques to set up **mirrored hard drives**. RAID level 1 also is called duplexed drives. *- 2 controllers*

- **RAID Level 2** introduced interleaving data across multiple drives for increased performance. It used **Hamming code** for error detection. Only specially designed hard drives could use RAID 2, so it was never used commercially.

- **RAID Level 3** uses data striping across multiple disks in parallel with an additional disk for parity error detection and recovery. RAID 3 is used for very high bandwidth applications. You can automatically recover from the failure of a single drive in a RAID 3 system.

- **RAID Level 4** is very similar to RAID 2 but manages drives independently instead of in parallel. RAID 4 was never commercially produced.

Hamming code is an error-correction code named for R.W. Hamming of Bell Labs. Various codes of varying complexities exist under the general title *Hamming code*. The simplest of these codes sends three check bits for every four data bits, enabling data checking of every seven bits and correction by using a simple calculation.

- **RAID Level 5** is the most popular implementation of disk arrays. It mixes data and error correction information across all drives. RAID 5 uses additional write overhead and is slower than writing to a single drive. High performance controllers with onboard RISC processors and large banks of cache memory are used to overcome performance limitations. RAID 5 drive arrays can suffer a single drive failure without data loss or interruption of operation.

- **RAID Level 6** operates similarly to RAID 5 but adds a second error encoding method. It allows failure of any two drives in the array without data loss or service interruption. Additional error encoding overhead makes RAID 6 slower than RAID 5. RAID 5 and 6 are preferred where transaction security is more important than performance.

Some manufacturers have described their products using a combination of RAID levels. For instance, RAID 10 is a combination of levels 1 and 0. RAID 53 is a combination of levels 5 and 3. Such classifications are for market positioning only and may have only a couple of proprietary improvements. The RAB is working to eliminate unsanctioned and confusing references to RAID levels. You can learn more about the RAID Advisory Board at their Web site at www.raid-advisory.com.

In 1994 the RAB began certifying RAID products to indicate full compliance with RAID level descriptions. It also defined a new set of standards called **Extended Data Availability and Protection (EDAP)**. EDAP more thoroughly and accurately defines the operational characteristics of drive arrays and systems. EDAP also is tightly controlled by the RAID Advisory Board to prevent market confusion.

EDAP classifications are as follows:

* **Failure Resistant**

    * *Regeneration* makes reliable online data available immediately in the event of a disk failure.

    * *Reconstruction* enables the contents of a failed disk to be reconstructed online and recorded on a replacement disk while maintaining acceptable application I/O performance.

    * Data protection in the event of a failure of any **Field Replaceable Unit (FRU)** in the storage system, I/O channel(s), and attached host(s).

    * Maintains consistency between data and its related redundant data.

    * Provides an indication in the event of a storage system failure.

* **Failure Tolerant**

    * Contains all failure resistant features.

    * Protects data in the event of power failure or overheating.

    * Upgrades storage system failure monitoring from an indication to a warning.

    * Supports disk hot swapping.

- Reliable, online data is available immediately in the event of the failure of any one storage system FRU, including device channels, controllers, cache, and power supply.

- **Disaster Tolerant**

  - Contains all failure resistant and failure tolerant features.

  - Supports the ability to attach to multiple I/O channels and multiple external primary power sources.

  - All FRUs (drives, power supplies, controllers, etc) are hot swappable.

  - Reliable, online data is available immediately in the event of a failure of any one zone in a multi-zoned storage system. This provides physical separation of the zones.

Removable Media Drives

Removable media drives allow you to remove a storage medium from your system when it is full and replace it with another disk or tape. Also available are removable drives, which are hard drives you can plug into and remove from a system. They function much the same way as the regular hard drives mentioned previously.

The **Bernoulli box**, named for Swiss scientist Daniel Bernouli, was introduced in 1983 by Iomega. Typically used on mainframe systems, Bernoulli boxes support removable magnetic media from 10 to 90 MB. Bernoulli boxes have a data transfer rate of 2.7 MB per second.

Removable media hard drives are popular due to the virtually unlimited storage capacity they allow. These drives do, however, have a typically slower data access speed than hard drives, but they are much faster than floppy disk drives. Typical removable media drives include Iomega JAZ and Zip drives, SyJet drives,

Sybase drives, APS drives, Bernoulli boxes, and others.

Removable storage drives designed for PCs handle cartridges that range from 40 MB to 2 GB, have read-write data transfer rates that range from 1.4 MB per second to 8.7 MB per second, with seek times of 12 ms. The drives range in price from $100 to $600, and removable media vary from $20 to $150.

It is a common error to not back up or duplicate data stored on removable media. If the media become damaged or unreadable, valuable data can be lost permanently.

Tape Backup Drives

Computer data has become a valuable and irreplaceable asset to most businesses. Failure of a hard drive or file server system can be costly. If you lose vital data, your business might not be able to continue operating. To protect company information from loss or malicious destruction, tape drives are used to make complete backup copies of vital files. Tape drives store huge amounts of information quickly. Tape backup drives for personal computers and computer networks usually are described by the type of interface port and recording technology used.

Industry surveys have found that 50% of companies that cannot recover lost data within ten business days never fully recover financially. Even worse, 93% of firms that lost vital data failed within 5 years according to a September 1994 issue of HP Professional.

Tape Drive Interface Ports

* **Parallel port interfaces** commonly are used to back up single PCs. If you install a tape drive on a single computer, you can connect the printer to a pass-through port on the drive to allow use of both the printer and the tape drive. Parallel port tape drives sacrifice backup speed for easy connections and portability.

 To combat slow backup speed, start the backup procedure at night so it will be completed before you need the computer again the next morning.

* **Floppy drive interfaces.** Although easy to install, this type of backup interface is very slow. Both parallel port and floppy drive interface tape backup designs are popular with small businesses with stand-alone PCs or small networks.

* **SCSI interface** internal or external backup tape drives offer the high performance required by most businesses when they must back up large amounts of data quickly or if interruption of computer use is costly.

* **USB interface** tape drives deliver the portability and ease of connection that parallel port and floppy interface backup tape drives feature, but with fast data transfer rates and hot swapping capability.

CD-ROM

A **CD-ROM**, or **compact disc – read-only memory**, drive reads only optical disks. Due to the increased storage capacity and relatively low cost, CD-ROMs have gained tremendous popularity in recent years. Originally a medium for music, CD-ROM was quickly adapted to storing computer data. A typical CD can contain 650 MB of digital data.

The low cost of manufacturing CD-ROM media makes it a popular way of distributing large databases, graphic files, and application software. The introduction of writeable, or recordable, CDs, known as **CD-R,** made it useful for data backup and archiving.

The original CD-ROM drive was designed to provide a constant rate of data transfer. To accomplish this, the CD medium spins faster when data near the center of the disk is read and slower when data near the outer edge is read. A 1X speed CD-ROM spins at 539 RPM when reading from the inner-most track and 210 RPM when reading from the outside track. The drive speed constantly adjusts in synchronization with the read head actuator. This is known as **constant linear velocity (CLV).**

 Speeding up the CD drive allows faster transfer of data – to a point. CD-ROM drives escalated in speed quickly as a marketing advantage over competing designs.

As CD-ROMs exceeded the 12X speed, the inertia of the CD disk made changing speeds difficult. Therefore, CD-ROM drives faster than 12X use a constant speed method known as **constant angular velocity (CAV).** Hard drives and floppy drives also use CAV. Because of CAV, data read from the inner tracks has a much lower transfer rate than data read from the outer tracks. On CDs, data is written first to the inside tracks, and fills the disk toward the outside tracks. Unless the CD-ROM disk is full, the highest transfer rate of new drives is never realized. The difference between the transfer rate of the inner-most track and the outer-most track is 60% slower. A 12X CD-ROM drive will perform as well as a 24X model with many CDs. The following table shows typical CD-ROM data transfer rates.

Drive Speed	Minimum Transfer Rate	Maximum Transfer Rate
1X (CLV)	150 KB/s	150 KB/s
2X (CLV)	300 KB/s	300 KB/s
4X (CLV)	600 KB/s	600 KB/s
6X (CLV)	900 KB/s	900 KB/s
8X (CLV)	1,200 KB/s	1,200 KB/s
10X (CLV)	1,500 KB/s	1,500 KB/s
12X (CLV)	1,800 KB/s	1,800 KB/s
16X (CAV)	930 KB/s	2,400 KB/s
20X (CAV)	1,179 KB/s	3,000 KB/s
24X (CAV)	1,400 KB/s	3,600 KB/s

CD-ROM Data Transfer Rates

CD-ROM drives are available with IDE or SCSI interfaces. For single-user desktop computers, the IDE interface offers good performance at an economical price. For multi-user, multimedia, or server operations, the SCSI interface offers fast data transfer for multiple concurrent requests.

CD-ROM drives feature an additional connection for a sound cable. The four-pin keyed cable plugs into the CD drive and sound card. The wires are very small and fragile. Be careful to insert and remove the cable by grasping the connector, not the cable.

DVD

DVD was originally *Digital Video Disc* and later *Digital Versatile Disc*. Today it is officially called *DVD*. DVD is optical disc storage you can use to store video, audio, and computer data. A DVD disc can store much more data than a conventional CD.

DVD was developed as a replacement for the video laser disk. As with CD-ROM, it became obvious that DVD was well suited to storing digital data. DVD-ROM drives became widely available in 1997, and each disk holds the equivalent of seven CD-ROMs.

Rewritable DVD became commercially available in early 1998. It features 120 ms access time for DVD-RAM disks and 85 ms data access time reading DVD-ROM.

DVD is *backward-compatible* to audio CDs, CD-ROMs, CD-R and video CDs. The following table shows the various capacities of DVD storage.

Drive Type	Sides and Layers	Data Capacity
DVD-ROM	Read-only 1 side, 1 layer	4.7 GB
DVD-ROM	Read-only 1 side, 2 layers	8.5 GB
DVD-ROM	Read-only 2 sides, 1 layer	9.4 GB
DVD-ROM	Read-only 2 sides, 2 layers	17 GB
DVD-R	Write-once, 1 side	3.9 GB
DVD-R	Write-once, 2 sides	7.8 GB
DVD-RAM	Rewritable 1 side	2.6 GB
DVD-RAM	Rewritable 2 sides	5.2 GB

DVD Data Storage Capacities

Write Once, Read Many (WORM)

WORM drives use initially blank CD recordable platters. Low cost platters are made of resin-coated polycarbonate plastic that contains a photosensitive dye. When intense laser light strikes the dye, the surface changes to be less reflective. Once written, data is permanent and cannot be altered. Humidity or magnetism does not effect WORM disks. They are well suited for archiving important data. High quality WORM media are platinum-coated to provide a minimum expected lifetime of 50 years.

Phase Change Optical Drives

Developed by Panasonic, phase change optical drives support 5.25"
rewritable optical media of 650 MB, 1.2 GB, 1.3 GB, 2.3 GB, and 2.6
GB capacities. It also supports WORM disk read and write operations.
Data transfer rates of 4 MB per second are possible.

Activity 4: Optimizing a Hard Disk Drive

To defragment your hard disk, complete the following steps:

1. At the DOS C: prompt, type **defrag** and press Enter. If you are using Window 95, run the Defragmentation utility in the Windows 95 System Tools folder.

2. Choose drive C and press Enter.

3. Choose to proceed with DEFRAG, change the optimization method, or exit.

4. When defragmentation is complete, choose the Exit option.

The next part of this activity demonstrates the use of the CHKDSK command to determine whether a hard disk has lost clusters. To detect and recover lost clusters, complete the following steps:

1. At the DOS C: prompt, type **chkdsk** and press Enter. If you are using Windows 3.11 or Windows 95, run ScanDisk, in the System Tools folder,

2. If the CHKDSK or ScanDisk utility detects lost clusters, it will ask if you would like to convert the lost chains to files. Type **y** and press Enter.

3. If you used ScanDisk, the utility automatically saved your lost clusters as recovered files. If you used CHKDSK, you must run the utility again, but this time you must type **chkdsk/f** and press Enter.

4. Recovered files are named FILE000.CHK, FILE0001.CHK, and so on in Windows 3.11 and in DOS. In Windows 95, they will appear as FILE000.TXT, FILE0001.TXT, and so on.

5. Delete the recovered files to free space on your hard disk.

Review

Hard disk drives store data and programs. You must physically format a hard disk drive before you can store data on it. Hard disk drives are formatted logically.

Read-write heads move across the **disk platter**, which is divided into tracks and sectors (the basic storage units). The same track on both surfaces is a cylinder. Hard disk drive interfaces are ST506, ESDI, IDE, and SCSI.

Disk access time is measured according to seek time and rotational latency. The data transfer rate is measured in MB per second. The actual speed of data transfer cannot exceed the computer's data bus speed.

Caching is used to improve hard disk performance. Both hardware and software caching are used.

Partitioning is used to divide disks into logical areas. Primary and extended partitions can be created. The **file allocation table (FAT)** contains information about where files are stored on a hard disk. Each file, regardless of its size, occupies at least one cluster. Large files can occupy multiple clusters; pointers connect each cluster to the next one to locate the entire file.

You can use various methods to optimize hard disk drive performance, including **defragmenting** the hard disk drive and removing lost clusters.

Floppy disk drives use removable media called **diskettes**. They are slower and have lower storage capacities than hard disk drives. Diskettes are either 5¼" or 3½" and can be double-density or high-density. Capacities vary according to these specifications.

Other types of drives include external hard disk drives, removable hard disk drives, and drive arrays.

LESSON 8: INPUT/OUTPUT DEVICES

This lesson describes the hardware devices used to make a computer fully functional. When you complete this lesson, you will be able to:

- discuss input/output ports, their uses, and cable restrictions.

- discuss monitor types, performance, and display modes.

- discuss keyboard options and features.

- discuss types of pointing devices and their relative advantages and disadvantages.

Input/Output Ports

The PCs on the market today have numerous types of ports where you can plug in the additional peripherals you purchase to go with your computer, such as a monitor, printer, mouse, and keyboard. The most common types of ports are serial, parallel, video, mouse, keyboard, game, and USB ports.

Serial Ports

Serial ports transfer data bits in a sequential, one-bit-at-a-time manner. Sending data bits in a single stream is an old technology, but still is used commonly. Serial communication is used mostly by modems, printers, terminals, and pointing devices. Modems use **synchronous** or **asynchronous** serial signaling methods. Printers, terminals, and other serial devices typically use asynchronous signaling methods. It is common for a PC to have two serial ports, often referred to as COM1 and COM2.

Synchronous refers to events that are synchronized, or coordinated, in time. For example, completing a current operation before the next operation begins is a synchronous event.

Asynchronous simply means not synchronous, or not coordinated.

The following figure shows a 9-pin serial port and a plug for the port.

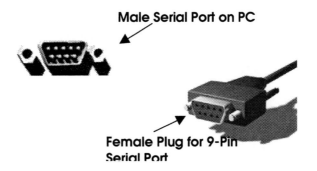

Male Serial Port on PC

Female Plug for 9-Pin Serial Port

Synchronous data transmission, because it must synchronize the sending and receiving of data, uses a more complex error detection known as *cyclic redundancy checking (CRC)*. The complexity of this system makes devices capable of synchronized transmissions more costly, but suggested for transmitting large amounts of data.

Asynchronous serial data transmission uses simple error checking to identify the start and end of the data packet. It also includes parity checking. A common serial data packet consists of one start bit, seven or eight data bits, one parity bit, and a stop bit.

Parity checking indicates that the sum of transmitted data is even or odd. If the data sum is different from the parity bit state when received, the destination device knows to request a retransmission of the bad packet. Parity checking will miss errors that involve two bits of data. Because most data errors involve only one bit, parity checking is considered adequate for most data transfers.

Serial connections are standardized by the EIA/TIA 232-E specification. Officially known as *Interface between Data Terminal Equipment and Data Circuit-Terminating Equipment Employing*

Serial Binary Data Interchange, it is commonly known by its older name: Recommended Standard 232 (RS-232). Established in 1969, the serial specification details connector types, signal levels, and connector pins that signals are carried on.

Both 25-pin and 9-pin male DB-style connectors are used to connect serial devices. Serial cables can be as long as 50 feet, but special shielding can allow reliable operation using cables longer than officially allowed. Typical transfer rates are between 110 bits per second and 115.2 KB per second.

Industry Standards

Many organizations set guidelines and/or review technologies in an attempt to standardize industry technologies. The following table shows some of these standards:

Standard	Emphasis	Format	Example
ANSI	Standardizes existing industry standards		X3.135
ITU-T	International communication standards	Letter.#	X.25
EIA	Electrical and electronics recommendations	RS-#-version EIA-#-version	RS-232-C EIA-485-A
IEEE	Develops new standards	IEEE-#.#	IEEE-802.3
ISO	International standards	ISO #	ISO 7498
TIA	Telecommunications Recommendations	TIA-#-version	TIA-568-B

Parallel Ports (Female)

Parallel ports are commonly used to connect printers to PCs They use a DB 25 female connector on the computer and a 36-pin Centronics (developed by Centronics Data Computer Corporation) female connector on the printer. The parallel port, also commonly called a Centronics interface, is usually referred to as LPT1.

The following figure shows a Female parallel port and a male parallel plug.

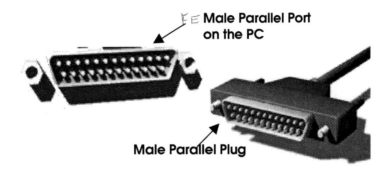

FE **Male Parallel Port on the PC**

Male Parallel Plug

Developed in the mid-1960s, parallel ports transfer eight bits of data in parallel at one time. Five additional control lines to and from the printer are also provided.

> **Tip** Note that the connector type on the PC is the same for 25-pin serial ports and for parallel ports, but the gender is opposite to prevent connecting the wrong type of device.

Data is transmitted in parallel much faster than in serial. 100 KB per second transmission rate is normal. However, parallel data must arrive at the destination at the same time to prevent timing errors. The longer the cable, the more unreliable parallel data becomes. Parallel cables must be kept short, usually under 15 feet, to provide reliable operation. High quality cables can be used to extend the maximum reliable distance, and parallel extenders are available to allow extended cable lengths. Extenders typically convert the parallel signal into serial form to send it hundreds or thousands of feet. The receiving converter then changes the serial signal back to parallel. This process sacrifices parallel port speed for greater distance.

 The Institute of Electrical and Electronics Engineers (IEEE) is an organization of engineers, scientists, and students of electronics and associated fields. The IEEE has more than 300,000 members and is involved with setting standards for computers and communications. The Computer Society of the IEEE is a separate organization, with more than 100,000 members.

Formalized as Institute of Electrical and Electronics Engineers (IEEE) 1284-1994, this standard enhanced parallel port operation in 1994 by including high speed bi-directional operation. Cable lengths are limited to 3 meters (about 10 feet) for type A and B traditional parallel ports and to 10 meters (about 33 feet) for the new type C high speed port. Type C parallel ports use a new 36-pin subminiature Centronics connector to prevent accidental connection to older parallel ports. Two new parallel port modes also were added to enhance printer support and add features for other devices.

- **Extended Capabilities Port (ECP)** adds support for new printers and scanners. This port offers the following features:

    ▶ data transfer speeds of 2 MB per second

    ▶ bi-directional, 8-bit operation

    ▶ ability to send data or commands over data lines

    ▶ support for CD-ROM and scanners

- ▸ **first in, first out (FIFO)** buffer to support higher data speeds

- ▸ support for data compression

- ▸ DMA support

- ♦ **Enhanced Parallel Port (EPP)** adds options required by non-printer devices such as CD-ROMs, tape drives, external hard drives, network adapters, etc. This port offers the following features:

  - ▸ data transfer rates as fast as 2 MB per second

  - ▸ bi-directional, 8-bit operation

  - ▸ support for multiple daisy-chained peripherals on a single port

  - ▸ uses programmed or interrupt-based I/O, but not DMA

Keyboard Ports

 Because the keyboard receives power through the motherboard connection, do not plug in or disconnect the keyboard while power is on.

PC keyboards connect to the computer motherboard with a **DIN connector** (named for the Deutsch Industrie Norm, the German national standards organization). Original PCs used standard ½" round DIN connectors keyed with five pins. The IBM PS/2 line of computers introduced keyboards with six pin $^5/_{16}$" mini DIN connectors. Both connector types are widely used, with the mini DIN style starting to become more common. Both styles can be adapted to the other size.

> Mini DIN connectors also are used for PS/2 style mice. Be careful to plug the keyboard connector into the keyboard socket. Plugging the keyboard into the mouse connector will not damage the keyboard but it will not operate.

Mouse Ports

Many motherboard designs include dedicated mouse ports. The mini DIN mouse connector typically is located next to the keyboard connector.

Game Ports

Many personal computers include a DB15 female analog interface port, also known as a game port. Joy sticks, flight controllers, game pads, and other analog signaling devices plug into the game port. A secondary game port can be added to use two similar devices simultaneously.

Universal Serial Bus (USB)

The universal serial bus (USB) is intended to replace all other external interface ports. As many as 127 peripherals can be connected to one PC using USB. USB provides tremendous advantages over previous technologies, including the following:

* carries power to peripheral devices to eliminate the use of additional power cords to each device

* provides hot swapping capability

- automates aspects of device initialization

- makes adding peripheral devices as simple as plugging them in

- the operating system loads and initializes device drivers when it detects the device on the bus.

 Microsoft's Windows 95 OSR2 release was the first operating system to support USB.

USB supports two data transfer rates. Slow devices such as modems, joysticks, and game pads operate at 1.5 MB per second. Fast devices such as scanners, digital cameras, and multimedia video use a 12 MB per second rate. Intelligent initialization of each device on the bus determines the rate the device needs. The following figure shows a USB plug.

USB Plug

 Firewire also is a high speed serial bus. It is designed for very high speed devices such as hard drives, CD-R drives, and full-motion video editing. It is a complimentary technology and is not intended to replace USB.

Video Ports

Video ports allow connection of the monitor to the computer. Video ports are either digital or analog.

- Digital video ports were originally used for monochrome, CGA, and EGA video signals. A DB9 female connector was used in the video interface card to plug in the monitor. This prevented accidental connection of serial devices that plug into a DB9 male connector.

♦ VGA and later video standards use an analog signal and a high density DB15 connector. The analog video port is the same size as the digital port but contains more contacts, or pins. The analog signal is completely incompatible with previous digital video signals.

The following figure shows a 15-pin video port and the plug for the port.

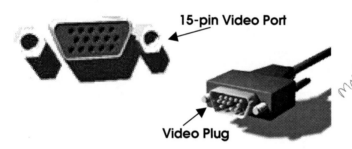

Check pins of the monitor cable if you lose color to your monitor

15-pin Video Port

Video Plug

Video Port and Plug

 Tip

Adapting the connector of a digital monitor to an analog video port will not work.

Some first generation analog monitors would accept digital video signals as well. The NEC Multisync monitor is an example of a monitor that can be adapted to a digital or analog signal.

Monitors

A **monitor** contains a **cathode ray tube (CRT)**, which consists of a large vacuum tube with a flat screen at one end and an electron gun at the other end. Electrons emitted from the gun strike phosphors on the surface of the screen, causing them to glow for a short time. Early monitors were **monochromatic**, meaning one color. Monochrome monitors displayed all amber, green, or white phosphors against a black background. The video display adapter card contains the digital-to-analog converter chip, memory, and other required control circuitry. Software interacts with the video display adapter card to convert digital signals from the CPU to the proper signal for the monitor to display.

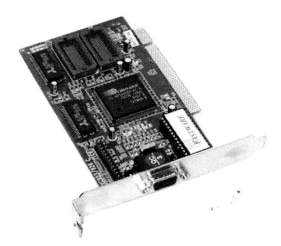

Video Display Adapter Card

Color monitors use three electron guns. Screens in color monitors contain small clusters of red, green, and blue phosphors. Electrons strike the screen with different intensities in different locations to produce different colors. Each dot displayed on the screen is a cluster containing a red, green, and blue phosphor dot. The electron beam must strike the correct color phosphor dot to produce the intended color. By striking combinations of color dots, other color combinations and hues are created. The distance between dots is called the dot pitch. The smaller the dot pitch number, measured in millimeters, the sharper the display image. A .39 mm dot pitch display is noticeably less sharp than a .28 mm dot pitch display, but monitors with a small dot pitch are more expensive to manufacture and purchase.

The size and resolution of the monitor you select directly impact viewing comfort. To best view information on your monitor, use the following table to help you determine the optimal resolution for your monitor:

Monitor	Resolution
14-inch	640x840, 800x600
15-inch	640x480, 800x600, 1024x768
17-inch	800x600, 1024x768, 1280x960
	1280x1024
20-or 21-inch	1024x768, 1280x960,
	1280x1024, 1600x1200,
	1600x1280

Refreshing the Screen

Refresh rate is a measure of how often the entire screen is redrawn to maintain a constant image.

Because phosphors glow for only a split second, the picture on the screen must be frequently redrawn or re-illuminated. The higher the refresh rate, the better.

An **interlaced** monitor requires two complete scans to redraw the screen. It redraws all the odd rows the screen on its first scan, then all the even rows on a second scan. This procedure sometimes causes a distracting flickering effect. If the monitor's vertical refresh rate is less than 60

Hz, the flickering is quite noticeable. Vertical refresh rates greater than 60 Hz minimize flickering.

 Interlaced display video cards and monitors are less complex to produce and less expensive than non-interlaced products. However, it can cause discomfort when viewing the monitor for an extended time, making it worth the extra cost to purchase the interlaced display.

Noninterlaced monitors redraw all rows of the screen on each scan, eliminating flickering, and producing a better quality picture. A noninterlaced monitor requires a video adapter that supports non-interlaced modes.

The following table shows the resolution of many common types of monitors.

Adapter	Maximum Resolution	Maximum Colors[1]	Monitor/Display Type
Monochrome Display Adapter (MDA)	720 x 350	1[2]	Digital monochrome/text
Color Graphics Array (CGA)	640 x 200	16	Digital RBG/text
	640 x 200	4	Digital RGB/graphics
Hercules Graphics Controller (HGC)	720 x 350	1[2]	Digital mono/graphics
Enhanced Graphics Array (EGA)	640 x 350	64	Digital RGB/graphics
Multi Color Graphics Array (MCGA)	640 x 480	16	Analog RGB/text
		256	Analog RGB/graphics
Video Graphics Array (VGA)	720 x 400	16	Analog RGB/text
	640 x 480	256	Analog RGB/graphics
XGA	1056 x 400	16	Analog RGB/text
	1024 x 768	65,536	Analog RBG/graphics
Super VGA	1024 x 768	256	Analog RGB/graphics
8514/A	1024 x 768	256	Analog RGB/graphics

[1] maximum colors and maximum resolution may not be simultaneously available
[2] black, white and intense white are displayed

Common Video Resolutions

Keyboards

A keyboard is the primary data entry device for personal computers. However, voice command and dictation technologies are rapidly becoming viable alternatives to keyboards.

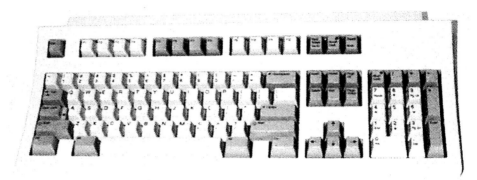

Standard 101-Key Keyboard

 Although the 101- or 104-key keyboard design is the most popular, other keyboard designs offer special purpose features. For example, the Microsoft Natural keyboard uses an ergonomic shape to minimize stress on users' wrists.

All keyboards produce false signals, or noise, when you press a key. A process called **debouncing** helps eliminate false signals. A microprocessor constantly examines the state of each key. Debouncing procedures verify that you pressed a key for at least two scans before sending a signal to the CPU.

Pointing Devices

Pointing devices, originally used for computer-aided design (CAD) and graphic design, are now essential tools for controlling the operation of almost every computer. A variety of pointing devices are on the market today, including the mouse, track balls, touch pads, pointing sticks, digitizing tablets, light pens, and touch screens.

Mouse

Relative-position devices move in relation to the last position. **Absolute-position devices** move in relation to a fixed, or absolute point.

The mouse is a **relative-position pointing device** that attaches to a serial interface, bus interface, mouse port, or USB port. You must install support software, called a **mouse driver**, before you can use a mouse. Some operating systems detect the mouse automatically and load the correct driver for you. Connecting a mouse to a dedicated mouse port still uses an I/O port address and interrupt, but more choices for these settings make preventing conflicts easier.

A serial mouse plugs into a serial port, typically COM1 or COM2. It is common to plug a serial mouse into COM1, using IRQ 4. A bus mouse uses its own interface card, freeing a serial port and providing additional IRQ choices. The bus mouse interface card requires one expansion slot, which may be in short supply, in the computer data bus. A mouse with a USB interface does not use an additional IRQ or serial port. Some mice use an infrared interface to eliminate the cord.

Two-Button Mouse

Types of Mouse Devices

Several types of mouse devices are on the market today:

- The **mechanical mouse** was the first generation of pointing devices. Doug Engelbart of Stanford Research Institute invented it in 1960. The mechanical mouse used two potentiometers connected to wheels set at 90-degree angles to measure movement. Because potentiometers tend to wear out quickly, this early mouse was not always reliable.

- The **optical mouse** was introduced to address the shortcomings of the mechanical mouse. The optical mouse emits a beam of infrared light that reflects off a special mirrored mouse pad with a checkerboard pattern. Changes in the reflected light, caused when the user moves the mouse over the special mouse pad, measure mouse movement. Optical mice have no moving parts for movement measurement and are quite reliable. Only the buttons on an optical mouse are subject to mechanical wear. The optical mouse requires a manufacturer-provided optical mouse pad to work properly. The mouse pad must be clean and undamaged, and the user must hold the mouse in alignment with the pad.

- The **optical-mechanical mouse** combines the reliability of the optical mouse and the ease of use of the mechanical mouse. A roller ball protrudes from the bottom of the mouse. The ball rolls against two interior spoked wheels set at 90-degree angles. A light shines through each spoked wheel. When the wheel moves, it interrupts the light and measures movement.

 The Microsoft two-button optical-mechanical mouse set the standard for reliable and inexpensive mouse devices. Because the roller ball is in contact with the desktop surface, dirt buildup inside the mouse can be a problem. Using a mouse pad decreases the dirt buildup problem and provides better traction. A dirty mouse causes the mouse pointer to jump or move erratically on screen when you move the mouse. Cleaning the mouse ball and internal rollers restores proper operation.

• The **strain gage mouse** also has no moving parts. Two electronic strain gages in the bottom of the mouse protrude to touch the desktop. Moving the mouse causes pressure on the gages, which is used to calculate mouse movement. No special surface is needed and no moving parts are present in the movement-measuring part of the mouse to wear out. Consequently, strain gage mice are extremely durable and do not need routine cleaning.

Other Relative-Position Pointing Devices

• **Track balls** are similar to a mouse turned upside down. The user moves the exposed ball with their fingers or thumb. Most track balls use the optical-mechanical design of their mouse cousins. Like mice, they become dirty and must be cleaned periodically. A track ball is best for small, crowded desk areas, because they are stationary and do not require as much room to operate as a mouse.

• **Touch pads** use solid state technology. A touch pad is stationary like a track ball and uses very little desktop space. Moving your finger around the surface of the touch pad moves the mouse pointer on the screen. Tapping the touch pad once or twice is the same as clicking the mouse button. The touch pad is an effective solution for laptop computers, but is also available for desktop computers. Touch pads sense the capacitance of the human touch. Touching them with a pencil or pen has no effect. The only maintenance required is periodic cleaning of the surface to keep it reasonably free of dirt and liquid.

- A **pointing stick** protrudes between the G, H, and B keys on the keyboard and is found mostly on laptop computers. By putting pressure on the stick, you move the mouse pointer on the display. The pointing stick allows users to keep their fingers on the keyboard while maneuvering the mouse pointer around the monitor screen.

Digitizing Tablets

Digitizing tablets are **absolute-position** pointing devices. The position of the **puck** or **stylus**, on the tablet surface corresponds to a specific position on the computer screen. Tablets range in size from that of a small mouse pad to the size of a drafting table.

You can use either a stylus or a puck with a digitizing tablet. A **stylus** is a pen-shaped instrument used to point to menu items. A **puck**, which resembles a regular mouse, may have a connection cord or may be wireless. You must periodically replace the batteries in wireless pucks, but you do not have to deal with a long cord. Pucks can have from four to sixteen different buttons to control options of the application software.

 Pucks are called pucks because early versions closely resembled hockey pucks.

Types of digitizing tablets include electromagnetic, resistive surface, and acoustic.

- An **electromagnetic digitizing tablet** has a wire grid beneath the surface. An electric field is sent across the grid at specific intervals and wires in the pickup coil of the puck cut the field, generating a pulse. This pulse is measured and converted into screen coordinates. Electromagnetic tablets are the most popular for CAD and graphics design applications.

- A **resistive surface digitizing tablet** uses a coated surface instead of a wire grid. The puck reads voltage differences induced into the surface. An analog signal from the puck or stylus identifies its location, which is converted into screen coordinates. Resistive surface tablets are commonly used to capture handwriting and signatures for security and credit card software.

- An **acoustic digitizing tablet** uses sound to locate the stylus, which generates a high voltage spark that travels across the tablet to two microphones. Triangulation is used to locate the position of the stylus. Sounds in the 65-75 KHz range are used to avoid environmental noise.

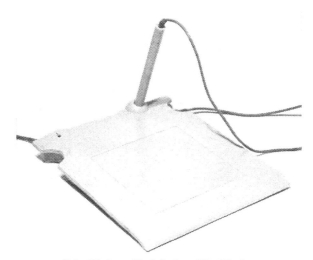

Digitizing Tablet with Stylus

Light Pens

Light pens resemble pens used for writing and are attached to the computer by a cord. The tip of the light pen contains a photo detector that, when placed on the surface of the monitor screen, detects the electron beam that passes by when the screen is refreshed. The light pen sends a signal to the computer and the signal computes the pen's coordinates. Light pens have tip switches that you can program like the buttons on a mouse. Light pens are useful for freestyle drawing and graphic design, but they have not become popular for general purpose use.

Touch Screens

♦   **Touch screens** are less precise than other pointing devices. They often are used in information kiosks, industrial control terminals, medical displays, point of sale terminals, and computer training because they provide an intuitive way for users to interact with the computer. A touch screen monitor is the same as any other monitor except for the additional touch detection surface and supporting interface electronics.

Review

Various types of hardware are required to support and customize computer operation.

Input ports such as **serial, parallel, keyboard, mouse, game, USB, and video** allow the connection of various external devices to a personal computer. USB is designed to replace all other external port types. **Serial communication** can be **synchronous** or **asynchronous**.

Monitors are the primary display device for personal computers. They are available in different sizes and support different display resolutions and color combinations.

Keyboards are used to control and enter data into computers. Several key layout designs have evolved, from 84 keys to 104 keys. Ergonomically designed keyboards are designed to make typing easier on users' wrists.

Pointing devices let you control graphical user interface operating systems and CAD or graphics design software without using the keyboard. The **mouse** is the most popular pointing device, **digitizing tablets, light pens, and touch screens** answer the specialized needs of many users.

LESSON 9: PRINTERS

After completing this lesson, you will be able to:

♦   install a printer

♦   identify different types of printers and their permanent and replaceable components

♦   explain the laser printing process

♦   discuss the replaceable components of a laser printer

♦   determine appropriate paper to use

♦   explain how paper is fed into various types of printers

♦   understand scanners

Installing a Printer

You can connect printers directly to a computer or via a network interface. Connecting a printer to a stand-alone computer requires a serial, parallel, or USB cable.

- **Serial printers** and many plotters use serial connections. The maximum length of a serial cable is 50 feet, but transfer speed is slower than other connection technologies. Serial connections require that both the sending and receiving devices are configured alike, with common bit, stop bit, parity, handshaking, and baud rates. Improper configuration of either device or an error in serial cable construction can result in no response or unusual operations.

- **Parallel printers** are the most popular type of printer due to a standardized interface and cable and easy setup. No special configuration is required for parallel printers connected to PCs. Some plotters are now using parallel interfaces.

- **USB printers** use cables as long as 5 meters (about 16 feet). Theoretically, you also can use a hub to extend the total USB cable length to 315 meters (1033 feet). Because USB was a defined standard before it was produced commercially, the cable and interface are consistent. Hot swapping features allow you to add or remove USB devices without first turning off the device or the PC. The USB printer and port do not require any configuration.

   Adding extensions to a USB cable can cause timing and low voltage problems that could compromise or damage USB devices.

- **Network printers** are standard printers with serial or parallel ports, which also contain an optional network interface. The network interface must be matched to the network protocol and cable type to operate properly. Printer network interfaces may be installed internally as a manufacturer or third-party option or as a separate box that plugs into both the network and the printer's parallel or serial port. Some stand-alone printer network interfaces support multiple printers. Network interface printers can be moved easily to anywhere a network cable connection is available. A computer located thousands of feet or even miles away from the printer can still print to it. Software supplied by the network operating system manufacturer directs print jobs destined for the PC's local printer port to the network printer instead.

Types of Printers

Printers are generally divided into impact and nonimpact technologies.

Impact printers have print heads that strike a page through a ribbon, leaving an imprint. These printers are used where multiple copies of the printed material are required or for very high speed printing.

Nonimpact printers use either a special process or a special print head that transfers toner or ink to the page. Good print quality, quiet operation, and generally economical cost make the nonimpact printer today's most popular type of printer.

Impact Printers

Line printers use several techniques to print an entire line of text across the width of a page at one time. Print speeds of 2,000 lines per minute, or approximately 32 pages per minute, are possible. Line printers are extremely rugged and operate well in dusty or hot industrial environments. They are used to print huge volumes of information. A line printer is extremely noisy, but is usually housed in a sound enclosure that is part of the printer case.

 You must replace the ribbon in a dot-matrix printer when it begins to wear out, causing light printed text. Printer ribbons are relatively inexpensive, often selling for only a few dollars.

Dot-matrix printers use a print head that travels back and forth across the paper width. As it moves, tiny wires in the print head strike the ribbon and paper to print characters. The print head relies on a permanent magnet that holds the print wires inside the head. A spring on the print wire pushes against the permanent magnet. The print wire is wrapped in a coil of wire that becomes an electromagnet when energized. The energized coil produces a magnetic charge that repels the print wire from the permanent magnet. When energy is removed from the coil, the spring retracts the print wire. This process is used to repeatedly fire the individual wire pins of a print head against the ribbon and paper to form printed characters.

The most common pin configurations on dot-matrix print heads are 9, 18, and 24 pins. Print quality increases as the number of wires in a print head increases: 9-pin print heads have a single row of print wires, and 18- and 24-pin print heads have two rows of print wires. You can produce *near-letter quality* characters using an 18- or 24-pin dot-matrix printer.

Nonimpact Printers

Ink-jet printers spray ink onto paper to create images. A 300 **dots per inch (DPI)** dot-matrix print nozzle is used to form high quality characters. Some ink-jet printers use a piezo-electric crystal that squeezes ink through the print nozzle by subjecting it to an electric current. Others use a heating element to boil the ink, developing steam that forces the ink through the nozzle. Early ink-jet printers had problems with clogged print head nozzles, and cleaning the print head was a delicate and messy task. Replaceable ink cartridges allow disposal of the actual print head to eliminate ink nozzle clogging. The addition of color printing combined with low equipment cost and low operating cost has allowed ink-jet printers to become more popular than dot-matrix printers for home and business use.

> **Tip** As you print, you consume the ink in the ink-jet cartridge. You must replace the cartridge when the print quality begins to fade. Ink-jet ink cartridges range in price from a few dollars to $50, depending on the type of ink and the brand of the printer.

Laser printers produce the highest quality output, compared to other types of PC and workstation printers. Laser printers work much like photocopiers, using an **electrophotographic (EP)** process, in which highly amplified light rays and heat transfer images to the page. Although some laser printers have advanced features, the basic functionality is common to all laser printers. The following list includes the basic components found on most laser printers.

◆ **Toner** is a fine powder consisting primarily of plastic (polymer), sand (silica), and rust (iron oxide). Laser printers use this finely powdered toner instead of liquid ink.

◆ The **toner cartridge** contains reservoirs of toner. It also contains the OPC drum and developer components in some laser printers.

◆ The **OPC drum** is a cylinder coated with **organic photoconductive (OPC)** material. The drum may be a separate component of the printer or may be contained in the toner cartridge. Exposure to light causes the surface to become electrically charged.

◆ The **fuser assembly** uses heat and pressure to bind the toner to the paper. The fuser assembly includes a top fuser roller, which provides heat, and a bottom roller, which provides pressure.

◆ The **rollers** are parts that mechanically advance the paper through the printer. The pick-up roller grabs the paper from the input paper tray.

- The **corona wire** is a thin wire that conducts electrical charges to the OPC drum or the paper.

- The **eraser lamp** is a light source that shines on the OPC drum to clear it of any previous electrical charges.

 Laser toner cartridges last longer than printer ribbons or ink-jet cartridges, but you must replace them eventually. They cost between $75 and $200, and most cartridges are available form office supply stores. Remember to check the make and model of your printer carefully; almost every model requires a different type of cartridge.

How Laser Printers Work

To print a page, a laser printer completes the following steps:

- **Receives information.** Computers communicate with laser printers using one of several industry-standard printer languages. The most common are Adobe's **Postscript®** and Hewlett Packard's **Printer Control Language (PCL)**. These languages describe whole pages of information to the printer. The printer stores these page descriptions in memory and waits until the computer sends the first end-of-page signal before it begins to print.

- **Cleans the drum.** Any toner left on the drum from printing the previous page is scraped from the drum surface by a rubber blade that looks much like a windshield wiper. The cleaning blade is normally inside the toner cartridge or OPC drum cartridge. Excess toner is retained in the disposable toner cartridge or dumped into a used toner collection bottle. You should dispose of used toner as the collection bottle fills. An eraser lamp exposes the OPC drum to a uniform light level that removes any trace of the previous image. This is analogous to applying a coat of primer to a wall before painting it another color.

If the laser printer has a toner collection bottle, never add used toner to the new toner hopper. Recycling used toner would be like adding a handful of dirt to your car's engine oil.

- **Conditions or charges the OPC drum**. The OPC drum rotates past the primary corona wire and receives a uniform negative charge across its surface. The OPC drum coating becomes electrically neutral, or an insulator, in the absence of light.

- **Writes the image**. A laser beam or LED assembly inside the printer writes the image onto the OPC drum by illuminating patterns of dots on it. The OPC drum surface becomes positively charged where light strikes it.

- **Develops or applies the toner**. As toner moves from the reservoir into the developer, it passes a strong magnet that energizes the toner with a negative magnetic charge. The developer unit contains the toner moving devices and the magnet. As the positively charged areas of the OPC drum that were exposed to light pass the negatively charged toner in the developer, opposite charges attract the toner from the developer to the OPC drum surface. The page image is *developed* on the surface of the OPC drum at this point. If the process were interrupted, you could read the text and see the graphics on the OPC drum surface.

- **Transfers toner to the page**. As the OPC drum rotates to receive the page image, paper advances to receive the toner. The paper passes over the transfer corona wire, which applies a strong positive charge to the paper. As the paper passes under the drum, the positive charge on the paper attracts the negatively charged toner from the OPC drum. At this stage, the page image toner is resting on the paper surface as a powder.

◆ **Fuses the toner**. Immediately after the printer transfers the toner to the paper, the toner is fused, or melted, onto the surface of the paper. The fuser assembly contains two rollers. The top roller has a heat lamp and the bottom roller applies pressure to the page. The combination of high heat and pressure fuses the toner to the paper.

Other types of nonimpact printers include dye sublimation, thermal wax, and solid ink. Except for laser printers, nonimpact printers are designed for graphic artists and small quantity printing of color graphics.

Ordinary black and white laser printers range in price from around $300 to more than $5000. The following table compares laser printers by price ranges.

Low End (under $400)
Output is usually 4 to 6 pages/minute
Recommended maximum load is 2000 to 6000 pages/month
600 x 600 dpi resolution
Homes and small businesses with no more than 10 or 15 employees

Mid-range ($400 to $1000)
Output is 6 to 10 pages/minute
Monthly maximum load is 12,000 to 20,000 pages
6000 x 600 dpi resolution
Businesses of less than 20 people

High End (over $1000)
Output is 12 to 24 pages/minute
Monthly maximum load is as many as 10,000 pages
At least 600 x 600 dpi; can range to 1200 x 1200 dpi
Ideal for large businesses
Usually handles large paper and multiple paper trays

Paper

The quality of output produced by a printer depends largely on the quality of the paper you use in your printer. Paper that absorbs ink too readily produces blurry images in ink-jet printers. Paper that has a glossy finish does not absorb ink quickly enough, causing the ink to smear or the toner to not fuse properly. Both ink-jet and laser printers will print on glossy paper, but you should be careful to use the paper designed for your printer.

 Printer manufacturers specify the size and thickness of acceptable papers. Using a paper size or thickness not supported by the printer design can lead to paper jams or printer damage.

- **Paper thickness** is normally expressed by its weight. A common paper used in office photocopiers and laser printers is 20-pound paper. 15-pound paper is noticeably thinner, and 40-pound paper is thicker. Some printers have an alternate straight-through paper path for thicker paper.

Paper weight is based on the weight in pounds of 500 sheets of 17x22.5" paper. This is called the paper **basis weight** and is noted on the paper package label.

- **Specialty paper** is available for ink-jet and laser printers. Special coatings on ink-jet paper provide much higher print quality than common copy paper. Similar specialty papers also are made for laser printers. Ink-jet and laser printer paper are not interchangeable. A coating that works well for liquid inks will cause poor print quality if you apply dry toner.

Printers such as thermal printers and fax machines require special paper. Without heat-sensitive paper, a thermal printer will not produce an image.

Paper Feeders

Printers use various methods to move paper past their print mechanisms. Laser and ink-jet printers have paper trays, and impact printers have pin, tractor, or friction feeders.

* Laser and ink-jet printers use **trays** that hold sheets of paper, which are fed by an internal paper transport system.

* Impact printers typically use **pin or tractor feeders** but also can use friction feeders. Pin and tractor feeders use fan-folded paper with perforated edges. The holes on the edges fit in sprockets on the feeder. The paper also is perforated horizontally so that individual sheets can be torn off after printing a page. Tractor feeders have sprockets that adjust to fit different widths of paper, but the width of pin feeders is fixed.

* Most impact printers have a lever you can move to apply pressure to the paper roller so you can feed individual sheets of paper through the printer.

Scanners

Although not the same as printers, scanners share some similar technologies. However, instead of sending output from a PC to a printer, you use a scanner to send input to a PC.

- **Flatbed scanners** are similar to copy machines, with a large glass surface where you place the item you want to scan, face down. The scanning head moves past the stationary document. Flatbed scanners provide generally high resolution images of individual documents. They are used when the quality of the scanned image is more important than the quantity of documents scanned. Multi-page document feeders are available for some flatbed scanners.

- **Drum scanners** are similar to laser printers but work in reverse, converting information on paper to electronic images. The scanning head on a drum scanner is stationary, and the document moves past the scanning head. Drum scanners are normally used where high volumes of documents must be scanned, but a low image quality is acceptable. *ex. copers*

- **Hand-held scanners** are moved over a stationary document by hand. They are inexpensive, compared to flatbed or rotary drum scanners, but produce low quality images. If a document is larger than the hand scanner, it must be scanned in strips that are later pasted together with a graphic editing program. Hand scanners are very portable and useful for quickly and inexpensively scanning small pictures and text that will be saved or pasted into a document.

ORC – optical

Flatbed Scanner

Scanner operation is relatively simple. The scanning head contains a light source and a series of sensors called **charge-coupled devices (CCDs)**. Light is reflected from the scanned document, with the sensors recording brightness. As the sensors read a line of information, the data is transmitted to the computer through an interface port. A stepper motor precisely controls the movement of the scanning head in a flatbed scanner and it controls document movement in drum-type scanners. Hand-held scanners have a tracking wheel that measures the speed of the scanner, and software compensates for the speed inconsistencies, placing each dot accordingly.

The quality of a scanned image can be limited in either of the following ways:

* Scanning a color photo with a monochromatic scanner results in a grayscale image. Gray tones in the scanned image may not correlate well to the colors of the original. For instance, a light red or pink shade will appear solid black in a gray scale image.

◆ Original documents of poor quality can produce unacceptable scanned images. The quality of an optically scanned image is always lower than the original. Minor imperfections in the scanned document are greatly accentuated in the scanned image. Time-consuming optical editing or rescanning may be required to obtain a good quality image.

Interfaces

Some inexpensive scanners have serial interfaces. Serial transmission of large amounts of data is very slow. Faster interfaces such as USB, SCSI, Hewlett-Packard's **general purpose interface bus (GPIB)**, or other proprietary interfaces offer better performance.

Beware of stand ard proprietary device

Installation

Scanners often include an interface card that must be installed and configured. As with any other interface in the PC, a unique IRQ, I/O address, and DMA channel must be identified and configured on the scanner card. A scanner with a USB interface benefits from high speed data transfer, with no need to configure another interface card.

Scanner interface software is required by some operating systems. Windows 95 can detect scanners and load the correct driver software automatically.

Review

Printers can be connected directly to a PC using a **serial, parallel**, or **USB cable**. Printers also can use a network interface.

Printers are classified as **impact** or **nonimpact**. Nonimpact printers use liquid or solid ink (thermal wax or dyes) to print. Laser printers use an EP process to transfer the image to paper.

Paper quality will affect printer performance as well as print quality.

Paper is fed through printers using **paper trays** (laser and ink-jet printers) or **pin, tractor**, or **friction feeders** (impact printers).

LESSON 10: MISCELLANEOUS HARDWARE

After completing this lesson, you will be able to:

* discuss modem features and operation

* discuss multimedia components such as sound cards and speakers

Modems

The word **modem** is derived from *MOdulator DEModulator* and converts digital signals from a computer into analog signals that are sent over phone lines. On the other end, another modem converts the analog signals back into digital signals.

Modems allow computers to communicate with each other over telephone lines. Data is transmitted synchronously or asynchronously and the transmission is measured by **baud rate** and **bit rate**.

Modems transmit data over full-duplex and half-duplex lines. A **full-duplex** line allows data to be sent and received at the same time on the same line. A **half-duplex** line allows data to be sent or received on the same line, but not at the same time. Modems use CRC and parity error checking to detect errors during transmission.

ex. phone conversation

ex. postcard

Baud rate is the number of discrete signal events per second in a data transmission, and **bit rate** is the number of bits a modem transmits in one second.

Remember, **synchronous transmission** is a method of sending data, characterized by regular time intervals between transmissions. **Asynchronous transmission** is a method of sending data that uses Start and Stop bits added to the message to assist the receiving modem in identifying the message being transmitted.

Baud is named for the French telegraph operator J.M. Emile Baudot (1845-1903), who developed a five-bit code for telegraphs.

Internal vs. External Modems

Two types of modems are available: **internal** and **external**. No matter which type you use, a telephone cable (RJ-11) connects the modem to the phone jack in the wall.

An **internal modem** is a card installed inside the computer, with telephone plugs outside. An **external modem** is a self-contained unit that connects to the serial or USB port on a PC.

Tip Plug a standard consumer telephone into a phone jack to test it. If you hear a dial tone, a PC modem will operate properly. If an office telephone works, but a consumer telephone will not, you need a phone jack that is wired differently.

→ ex phone extension

A PC modem connects to an analog telephone jack. Many private branch exchange (PBX), or digital, phone systems support multi-station telephones. If a modem is connected to a multi-station telephone jack, it will not operate.

Plugging a PC analog modem into a new style digital telephone line will damage or destroy the modem. Unfortunately, digital and analog telephone lines look alike.

Modem Speeds

PC modems were introduced in 1981, and data transfer rates have been increasing since then. The following table lists common modem speeds, although few 300-baud modems exist today, and faster modems, which transfer at speeds faster than 33,600 bits per second, are becoming more common.

Modulation Methods	Data Rate (bits/s)
Bell 103	300
Bell 212A	1,200
V.22bis*	2,400
V.32	9,600
V.32bis	14,400
V.34	28,800
V.34bis	33,600

Common Modem Speeds

* Bis means second version - literally encore in French

Modems can be made to operate faster than their rated speeds using various data compression techniques.

The **universal asynchronous receiver transmitter (UART)** chip on the serial card also affects modem speeds. Faster modems require faster UART chips. The UART converts parallel data from the PC data bus to the serial form needed by the serial port. Early UART chips buffered only one byte of data. Data rates above 9,600 baud would overrun the UART capacity to convert and move received data to the PC data bus. The 16550 UART provides higher speed operation, partially due to a 16-byte buffer. Communication software must support the faster UART design to take advantage of its advanced features. Older communication software will operate a fast 16550 UART in the slower backward-compatible mode.

Fax Modems

Fax modems combine the ability to transmit binary data to other computers and graphic images to other fax machines. The receiving fax machine can be a stand-alone fax machine or another fax modem in a personal computer. Because most of the document quality is lost during the optical scanning process, fax transmissions from computer to computer produce very good images. Most current generation modems include fax capabilities, and **direct inward dial (DID)** codes allow automatic routing of fax images through e-mail. **Optical character recognition (OCR)** software allows conversion of a graphical fax image into text. However, successful conversion from a graphic image to text depends on the quality of the received fax image.

Testing the Modem

Five factors affect the function of external modems: the modem cable, the modem power supply, the modem itself, the port, and the software. Internal modems do not have cables or power supplies, eliminating two possible sources of problems. Communications software configuration problems can cause the following problems:

- inability to connect to another computer

- connecting, but receiving garbled data

- no monitor display of what is entered at the keyboard

- two characters displaying for every one entered on the keyboard

You use communications software to change modem settings. The sending and receiving computers are not required to have the same software in order to communicate. Newer communications software tests the connections between modems for you, but most older software requires that you perform some or all the testing manually. For example, if you cannot connect to another computer, you can use the following command to verify that both modems are communicating at the same speed.

&Nx, where *x* is between 0 and 9

The *&Nx* command determines the modem connect speed. Using *&N0* allows the modem to determine the highest possible connect speed. The following table shows the commands for setting connect speeds.

Command	Connect Speed
&N0	Variable
&Nl	300 bps
&N2	1200 bps
&N3	2400 bps
&N4	4800 bps
&N5	7200 bps
&N6	9600 bps
&N7	12 Kbps
&N8	14.4 Kbps
&N9	16.8 Kbps

Modem AT Command Set

When PC modems were introduced in 1981, they included a set of commands called the AT command set, which was written to control the functions of the modem. The AT command set eventually became an industry standard and

AT stands for **Attention**.

was sufficient to control low speed modems. Higher speed modems use the AT command set with extensions. Unfortunately, the extensions are not standardized, so different manufacturers use different extensions. The following table shows the basic AT command set:

Command	Function
ATA	Tells the modem to answer an incoming call.
ATDT	Tells the modem to get a dial tone. To dial a number, type ATDT, followed by a phone number.
ATDL	Redials the last number dialed.
ATDL?	Displays the last number dialed.
ATEO	Turns local echo off.
ATEI	.Turns local echo on.
ATFO	Turns half-duplex on. Your modem will echo a copy of the data that it is transmitting.
ATFI	Turns full-duplex on. If the remote modem is echoing, your modem will display the information that the remote is receiving.
ATHn	Tells the modem to hang up. This command has a default value of ATH0. To take the phone off the hook, use the command ATHI.
ATIn	Displays information about the modem. *n* represents a digit between 0 and 9.
ATI0	Retrieves the product code.
ATII	Retrieves results of the ROM Checksum.
ATI2	Retrieves results of the RAM test.

Command	Function
ATI3	Retrieves product identification.
ATI4	Retrieves current modem settings.
ATI5	Retrieves NVRAM settings.
ATI6	Displays link diagnostics.
ATI7	Retrieves modem configuration.
ATI8	Reserved.
ATI9	Retrieves call duration.
ATLn	Controls the volume of the modem's speaker. Use 0 or 1 for low, 2 for medium, and 3 for high. The default is 2.
ATMn	Controls the speaker. n=0 turns the speaker off; n=1 turns the speaker on until the carrier is established (default setting); n=2 turns the speaker on; n=3 turns the speaker on immediately after the last digit is dialed and a carrier is established.
ATQn	Quiet mode suppresses display of result codes. Quiet mode is normally inactive. n=0 displays result codes; n=1 suppresses result codes; n=2 suppresses results in the answer mode.
ATSr=n	Sets values in the registers. r specifies the register number, and n specifies the value placed in the register. Modems using extended command sets may have non-standard registers. See modem documentation for details.
ATSr?	Retrieves the value in the register specified by r.
ATVn	Returns result codes as either character strings or numeric values. n=1 to display character string codes such as OK or NO CARRIER. n=0 displays numeric result codes.

Multimedia Personal Computers (MPCs)

Microsoft set minimum standards for multimedia PCs in 1991. These standards have been revised and are now called **MPC II**. To meet MPC II, the computer must have the following minimum capabilities:

- 80486SX or more powerful CPU *Pentitum I or II*

- 4 MB of RAM *16 RAM*

- 3.5" high density floppy disk drive

- 160 MB hard disk drive *5 G*

- CD-ROM drive with the following characteristics:

  - power consumption less than 40% of the CPU's power

  - average access time of one second or less

  - data transfer rate of at least 300 KB per second

- VGA monitor

- enhanced 101-key keyboard

- two-button mouse

- one serial and one parallel port

- musical instrument digital interface (MIDI)

- a 16-bit sound card

- Windows 3.0 or later version

- multimedia extensions for DOS

- speakers or headphones

Upgrading

You can upgrade a PC to an MPC by installing additional components. Multimedia kits are available that include a CD-ROM drive, a sound card with interface, and speakers. Before upgrading a PC, complete the following steps:

- Check the minimum PC hardware requirements listed previously.

- Determine whether upgrading is cost-effective.

- Check for an open slot on the motherboard for the sound card.

- Back up the CONFIG.SYS and AUTOEXEC.BAT files, because they will be changed by multimedia installation programs.

- Check the interrupt settings to determine whether an IRQ is available.

Resolving IRQ Conflicts

On older systems, you might have to resolve IRQ conflicts manually. You should first back up the CONFIG.SYS and AUTOEXEC.BAT files. You might need to change the order of the statements in these files to make devices work properly, especially SCSI devices. If possible, use diagnostic software to determine existing interrupt settings. Some interrupts from 9 to 15 probably will be available on 16-bit machines. Multimedia kits often include configuration managers to make installing devices easier.

> *Tip* Refer to the table in *Lesson 12: Troubleshooting* for a list of IRQs and their uses.

Sound

A computer must have sound capabilities to comply with MPC standards; therefore, you must install a sound card. Speakers are required in order to produce voice or music. Creative Labs Sound Blaster has become the standard in the sound card industry.

 To produce multimedia presentations or add voice to your documents, you need recording capabilities; otherwise, playback capabilities are sufficient.

You can store recorded sounds in an 8-, 16-, or 32-bit format. The 8-bit format is capable of 256 sound levels and the 16-bit format is capable of 65,536 levels. You need a 16-bit sound card to comply with the MPC standard. Sounds stored using 16-bit sampling require more disk space than sounds stored using 8-bit sampling.

Sound Card

Consider the following when buying a sound card.

Is the pin configuration 16 or 8?
Is an expansion slot available?
Does the card include drivers?
Is the card Sound Blaster-compatible?
Does the card support FM and MIDI sounds?
Is the card capable of recording sounds?
You must add speakers to use the sound card.

Computer speakers are magnetically shielded to protect magnetic media from accidental magnetic erasure and magnetization of the monitor or distortion of its display. Standard audio speakers are not magnetically shielded. Their magnets will cause strange color changes and distorted monitor display. This is a problem only if the speakers are in close proximity to the monitor or where you store magnetic media. If the monitor is distorted by a magnetic field, removing the magnetic field source (unshielded speakers) should correct the problem. If color distortion remains, degauss the monitor. Many monitors have manual degauss buttons among the front controls. Some monitors degauss automatically when turned on. If the color distortion does not return to normal within a week, manual degaussing performed by a monitor technician will correct the problem.

You should leave the speakers plugged into the sound card to prevent damage to the card.

Review

Microcomputers use **modems** to communicate over telephone lines. Communications can use either **synchronous** or **asynchronous** transmissions over **full-duplex** or **half-duplex** lines.

Modem speeds are measured by **baud rate** and **bit rate**. Modem communication is error-checked using CRC and/or parity error checking. Some modems include fax capability. Modem operation is controlled by the **AT command set**.

Multimedia hardware includes a CD-ROM drive, sound card, and speakers. Multimedia kits are available to upgrade a PC to an **MPC**, or **Multimedia Personal Computer**.

Speakers for computers shield magnetic fields common to all speakers. **Unshielded speakers** can erase magnetic data or distort the monitor's picture or color.

LESSON 11: LOCAL AREA NETWORKS (LANS)

After completing this lesson, you will be able to:

- describe how LANs are used

- explain the differences between peer-to-peer and client/server LANs

- describe LAN topologies

- describe the Ethernet, Token Ring, and ARCnet protocols

- explain the different uses of twisted-pair, coaxial, and fiber-optic cabling

How LANs Are Used

Local area networks (LANs) allow microcomputers to exchange data, or communicate, through a system of cabling and communication among hardware, devices, and software. LANs also allow microcomputer users to transfer data electronically rather than manually exchanging diskettes.

A **LAN,** or **local area network**, is a group of computers in a small area connected so that all systems can interact. A LAN usually includes PCs and shared resources such as printers and a server.

In most office environments, it is more efficient for users to share data. For those using network resources, working on a LAN offers the following advantages:

* sending, receiving, and printing data files (also known as data transfer)

* backup of data files, which is provided by network operations

* security, which is provided by a password and audit system

* program installation and maintenance

History of LANs

Terminal emulation uses one computer to simulate the type of terminal required to gain access to another computer.

LANs evolved because organizations realized that it was more cost effective for users to share resources. The first attempts to share resources added **terminal emulation** to personal computers. PCs could access mainframe data and system printers as well as PC-based programs and locally attached printers. Reports could be imported into a PC spreadsheet for analysis instead of being hand-typed into the spreadsheet from a printed report.

The first PC LAN allowed hard disk and printer sharing. Novell introduced NetWare in 1983. The first NetWare server ran on a proprietary Novell computer that used a Motorola microprocessor. It supported as many as 16 PCs connected through their serial ports. NetWare was expensive: approximately $12,000 for a four-user version. Later, advanced NetWare software ran on an XT computer and used proprietary network interface cards. Early Ethernet interface cards cost over $1000 each. Since then, costs have declined dramatically, and the number of LANs has increased significantly.

LAN Types

LANs use either peer-to-peer or client/server architecture or a combination of both.

Peer-to-Peer Networks

Peer-to-peer networks generally have the following characteristics:

- Users share files on their hard disks with each other, and data does not pass through a central server.

A **peer-to-peer network** is a network of at least two PCs connected directly to each other. Every computer is a peer, or equal, and no server is required.

- Resources such as data files, printers, and CDs, are spread among many peers. Failure of one computer will not affect the entire network, only the resources on the failed system are unavailable.

- No server machine is required in a peer-to-peer network; you can use regular desktop PCs.

- Access to shared resources usually is slower than in a client/server network or on a stand-alone computer, because a peer-to-peer network operating system cannot provide desktop and network access as efficiently as a dedicated server can.

- Peer-to-peer networks lack the sophisticated management and tracking capabilities of client/server systems, but peer-to-peer networks are economical and easy to install.

- Security is minimal, because each user decides which files, directories, drives, and other resources to share.

- Individual users may fail to back up critical data regularly. The value of company data might justify a client/server network.

- Peer-to-peer networks can coexist with client/server networks.

- Peer-to-peer networks are effective in small groups, but security and reliability issues become overwhelming on larger networks.

 Multiple-user access to a shared resource or data file is managed by the network operating system. Users may be tempted to purchase less expensive single-user software to use on a peer-to-peer network. Multiple-user access to a single-user program can corrupt data. No network operating system can prevent improper use of software; the operating system can enforce single-user access to a data file only through file locking.

The following figure illustrates a typical peer-to-peer network.

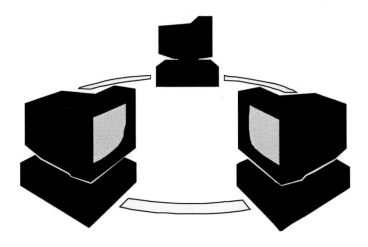

Three PCs Connected on a Peer-to-Peer Network

Windows 95 and Windows NT Workstation can be used as peer-to-peer network operating systems. LANtastic, Personal NetWare, and Windows for Workgroups are examples of DOS-based peer-to-peer network operating systems.

Client/Server Networks

Client/server networks generally have the following characteristics:

A **client/server network** involves two components: a **front-end client** and a **back-end server**. Each client is a fully functional stand-alone PC. The server is a PC, minicomputer, or mainframe that makes programs, files, data, and resources available to clients and provides administration and security to all systems on the network.

- Users work at computers that have independent processing capabilities. Some users need powerful computers, but less powerful computers are adequate for others.

- A server provides shared resources such as centralized file storage, printer sharing, database access, and network management. The client computer runs applications using resources available on the server. In other words, servers provide network services, and clients request network services.

- Specialized server equipment can be optimized to access data quickly. The high cost of specialized equipment can be spread among all users of the network.

- Centralized administration of a network from dedicated servers is more efficient and makes it easier to protect valuable company data.

- A server failure can result in the loss of significant amounts of company data, making backup extremely critical. Servers frequently use fault tolerant or redundant systems to minimize the potential for catastrophic loss of data, and an administrator rather than individual users handle backups.

+ Centralized servers can be overloaded with simultaneous requests for services.

+ File servers and database servers are the most common applications on a server, but some servers also provide dedicated communications and print services.

Banyan Vines, Digital Equipment Corporation Open VMS, Microsoft Windows NT Server, and Novell IntraNetWare are examples of client/server network operating systems. The following figure shows an example of a client/server network.

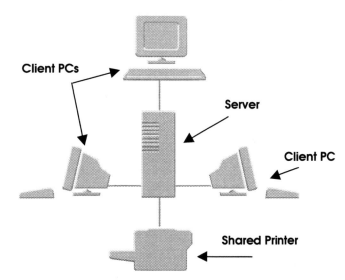

A Client/Server Network with a Shared Printer

LAN Topologies

A **topology** describes the network path used to transfer data from the data source to its destination. Following is a list of the most common topologies:

A **topology** is the configuration of the connections between LAN devices.

- The **bus topology** uses a single cable to connect all workstations in a daisy-chain fashion. All workstations share a transmission cable, but only one workstation at a time can transmit or receive data. Various methods, known as **protocols**, are used to enable orderly communication on a shared bus. Signals are broadcast to all stations on the bus, but each transmission is addressed to an individual workstation or server. Every workstation on the bus must receive and examine every transmission. The transmission is discarded by every workstation that it is not addressed to.

Bus topologies are easy to install and use the least amount of cable of any design. It can, however, be difficult to reconfigure this type of network as you add new computers, and it is the most difficult topology to troubleshoot. A cable break or bad connection anywhere in the cable shuts down the entire network. Intermittent bus failures can require expensive test equipment and skilled technicians to troubleshoot and isolate the bad connection.

The following figure shows a typical bus topology.

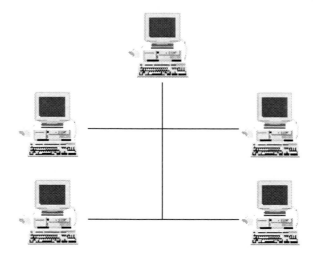

Typical Bus Topology with 5 PCs

- The **star topology** uses a **hub** as a central connection point, with each workstation connected to the hub by its own cable. Signals are broadcast to all workstations or can be passed from one station to another, depending on the protocol used. Star topologies can be more difficult to install than bus topologies. You must run an individual cable from the nearest hub to each computer. Therefore, the star topology uses more cable than any other type. Adding new computers is easy, because running a new cable to the computer is all that is required. Star topologies are also the easiest to troubleshoot. If a cable to a workstation has a problem, only that one computer is affected. If the cable to a hub is damaged, all uses of the hub are affected. The failure of all computers connected to one hub makes isolating the problem obvious. In some topologies, additional hubs can be connected to form a network with a distributed star topology.

The following figure shows a typical star topology.

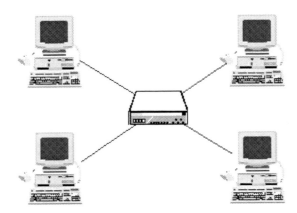

Typical Star Topology with 4 PCs and a Central Hub

♦   The **ring topology** uses a series of cables, or a ring, that forms a
closed loop. Signals pass from one device to the next on the ring.
Each network interface on the ring receives a transmission and
decodes it to examine the destination address. If the message is not
intended for that computer, the message is retransmitted to the
next computer in the ring. Each computer acts as a repeater,
allowing you to build large rings. Hubs, concentrators, or multi-
station access units (MSAUs) are used to connect computers to the
ring with drop cables.

The complexity of network interfaces has kept ring topologies
relatively expensive as other designs have fallen dramatically in
price. Rings are easy to install, depending on the size. Rings use
more cable than a bus, but less than a star. Rings become harder to
reconfigure as the number of attached computers increases. When
the maximum ring length or maximum number of computers on a

ring is reached, rings must be broken into multiple rings and bridged or routed together.

Troubleshooting a ring is aided by automatic diagnostic procedures performed by each computer on the ring. If the ring is broken, the upstream and downstream computers will send notifications to a ring monitoring unit about the problem and its location. Most ring topologies incorporate some type of fault tolerance to respond to ring breaks. One technique is to reverse the signal at the last computer on a broken ring and send the data back the other way. Another technique is to use dual rings. If one ring is broken, a station connected to both rings reroutes traffic onto the other ring. Dual rings also can provide automatic load balancing between rings. Ring topologies are difficult to plan. Technicians specifically trained in ring design are often necessary to plan and maintain large rings. Error tolerance makes ring topologies ideal for some networks despite their high cost.

The following figure shows a typical ring topology.

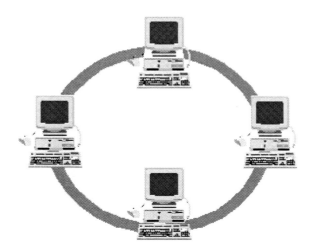

Typical Ring Topology with 4 PCs

Network Protocols

Protocols determine the way computers on a network communicate. They are like different languages spoken by computers. For a workstation and a file server to communicate, both must use the same protocol. Common LAN protocols include Ethernet, Token Ring, and ARCnet.

Ethernet

Throughput is the speed of processing data. A typical measure of LAN protocols is the bit rate, which is a measure of throughput. This is the bits-per-second data transfer rate supported by the channel.

Ethernet is a registered trademark of its developer, Xerox Corporation. The original Ethernet protocol was patented in 1975 and operated at 3 MB per second. A faster 10 MB per second Ethernet version 2 was developed in 1980 in a joint effort among Digital Equipment Corporation, Intel, and Xerox. Also known as DIX Ethernet, Ethernet II remains the standard protocol used on the Internet. The IEEE formalized the industry standard as IEEE 802.3. A newer and slightly different version of Ethernet was adopted by the **International Organization for Standardization (ISO)** as Ethernet 802.2. The IEEE 802.3 standard was adopted later by the ISO also. Ethernet is capable of 10 MB per second or 100 MB per second throughput.

The **media access method** consists of rules that determine which stations can access the cabling and when access can occur. Ethernet uses **carrier sense multiple access with collision detection (CSMA/CD)** or **carrier sense multiple access with collision avoidance (CSMA/CA)** as its media access method.

* **Carrier sense** means that all devices monitor the cable to determine whether the cable is already in use. If a transmission is occurring, other stations must wait to send data.

* **Multiple access** means that any station can use the cable.

* **Collision detection** is a process of announcing when a data collision has occurred. If two stations listen to the cable and do not hear any transmissions (carrier sense), they may try to transmit at the same time. Simultaneous data transmissions by two or more stations result in a garbled combination of all data. This is known as an **Ethernet collision**.

  The first computer to receive a garbled transmission sends a Jam packet to alert all stations on the cable that a collision has occurred. Stations involved in a collision will wait a random period of time and try again. Collisions are common in Ethernet; the number of collisions increases as the amount of network traffic increases.

* **Collision avoidance** is similar to collision detection, except that a small request to send a data packet is sent before the data, to minimize collisions. When a station wants to send data on the network cable, it first listens (carrier sense), then sends a small request to send the full packet to the intended destination. If two stations try to transmit at the same time, only the requests to send packets collide. If the destination station replies that it received the request to send packet, it is safe to send the data. Any station that hears the request to send or clear to send reply will know the cable is busy and will not collide with the data transmission. This sounds like a better idea than collision detection, but it requires additional transmission overhead. Even if only two computers are on a network, they still must go through the *request to send* and *clear to send* exchange before every data packet transmission.

The two popular types of Ethernet are **coaxial** and **twisted-pair**.

[handwritten note in left margin: 10 mega bit per seconds]

- ◆ **Coaxial (coax) bus Ethernet** topologies were the first available. They quickly gained a reputation for being temperamental and unreliable.

    – **10Base5 Ethernet** uses thick coaxial cables that can extend as far as 500 meters per segment. Repeaters can extend the total length of the cable to 2.5 kilometers.

    – **10Base2 Ethernet** uses thinner coaxial cable in lengths of 185 meters. With repeaters, the total length of a 10Base2 cabling can be 925 meters. Both coaxial bus topologies require a terminator at each end of the cable. Lack of termination or disconnection of any part of the cable will cause the entire network cable segment to fail.

- ◆ **10BaseT Ethernet** introduced the star topology and its inherent reliability and ease of troubleshooting. It was not until 10BaseT became widely available that small businesses could afford to use Ethernet. It uses **unshielded twisted-pair (UPT) cable**, which is inexpensive but offers little protection from electromagnetic interference (EMI). Incorrect wiring of 10BaseT cabling when installed is a common and very difficult error to find. Bad cables operate slowly and cause intermittent network errors. 10BaseT cables can extend 100 meters from the hub to the computer. Hubs can be connected to form a network 500 meters long.

 The naming convention used in 10Base2, 10Base5, and 10BaseT is an abbreviation of the specifications. For example, 10Base5 means 10 megabits per second (Mbps) throughput, a baseband network, with a maximum segment length of 500 meters.

Ethernet is now the most popular network protocol. The following table lists the most common implementations.

Implementation	Cable Type	Throughput	Transmission	Max Length
10Base5	Coaxial	10 Mbps	Digital	500 meters
10Base2	Coaxial	10 Mbps	Digital	185 meters
10BaseT	Twisted-pair	10 Mbps	Digital	100 meters
10Broad36	Coaxial	10 Mbps	Analog	3600 meters
10BaseF	Fiber-optic backbone	10 Mbps	Digital	2000 meters
100BaseX	Twisted-pair	100 Mbps	Digital	100 meters

Common Ethernet Implementations

Token Ring

The IEEE 802.5 committee published a standard in the early 1980s for token-passing ring networks. IBM marketed the first Token Ring network in the mid-1980s, which ran at 4 Mbps. In the 1990s, IBM introduced 16 Mbps Token Ring.

Only the number of computers in the ring affects each computer's cable access. Collisions do not occur, allowing a consistent data transfer rate. Although the original 4 Mbps Token Ring allowed only one token on each ring, today's 16 Mbps Token Ring allows multiple tokens on the ring at one time.

The Token Ring network derives its name from the communication method, which uses a token. The **token** is a special packet of information that controls access to media. A station that wants to use the cable must wait until it receives a token without data already attached, called a **free token**. After the station has transmitted its data and received a return delivery confirmation, it must release the token so another station can use it.

No electricity

Though the network configuration of the Token Ring looks like a physical star, internally, signals travel in a ring from one station to the next.

Workstations connect to a central hub called a **multi-station access unit (MSAU)**. MSAUs are connected through ring-in and ring-out ports to extend the ring. An electrical relay or circuit inside the MSAU adds each computer to the ring when the network interface requests a ring insertion and removes each computer from the ring when turned off. The integrity of the ring is automatically maintained by the MSAU and self-test diagnostics built into the network interface cards. A network interface card can remove itself from the ring if it senses an internal error.

Tip MSAUs are commonly, but incorrectly, called MAUs.

The ring can connect as many as 250 computers. The maximum ring length is 100 meters; however, both the number of computers in a ring and the ring size depend on so many different factors that it is impossible to state accurate limits. Each ring must be designed based on the type of cable, the length of the drop cable from the MSAU to each computer, and the MSAU and network interface card manufacturers. Different manufacturers design their equipment to different specifications. Due to the liberties manufacturers have taken to improve Token Ring, it is wise to choose one manufacturer for all parts of a Token Ring network.

Token Ring is widely used by companies that must connect LANs to a minicomputer or an IBM mainframe. The following table describes the types of cabling used in IBM Token Ring networks.

Cable Type	Internal Design
1	Two shielded twisted-pair 22 AWG wires
2	Two shielded twisted-pair 22 AWG wires for data and four twisted-pair 26 AWG wires for voice
3	Two unshielded twisted-pair 22 or 24 AWG wires
5	2 strands of fiber-optic cable
6	Two shielded twisted-pair 26 AWG wires for patch panel and wiring closet use
8	Shielded twisted-pair 26 AWG wire for use under carpets
9	Shielded twisted-pair 26 AWG, plenum-rated, fire-safe wire

Plenum refers to the design of air conditioning systems commonly used in commercial buildings. Room air returns to the air conditioner above the ceiling. An open grill in a false ceiling usually indicates a plenum air system. Flammable materials are not allowed in a plenum. The use of less expensive, but flammable cables in a plenum is a serious fire code violation.

ARCnet

The **Attached Resource Computing Network (ARCnet)** was developed by Datapoint in 1977 and is licensed to other companies. ARCnet was the first network interface protocol to provide compatibility between different manufacturers' products. ARCnet was formalized as the ANSI 878.1 standard, but it never received IEEE or ISO endorsement.

ARCnet uses a token-passing distributed star network topology. Coaxial cable connects hubs to computers and to other hubs. The original transmission speed was 2.5 Mbps, but enhanced or turbo ARCnet is rated at 4 Mbps. Although ARCnet is considered slow, it is a token-passing protocol, and the transmission speed is consistent. A heavily loaded ARCnet network can outperform a moderately loaded Ethernet network.

> ARCnet Plus is a 20 Mbps version that is backward compatible. Its delay in reaching the market allowed 10BaseT Ethernet and 100 MB Ethernet to become popular in the small business market.

The use of active hubs allows distances between the hub and computer as great as 2,000 feet. Passive hubs split the signal and decrease the distance from the passive hub to a computer to 100 feet. You can add active hubs to other active hubs (but not to passive hubs) to reach another 2,000 feet. The maximum cable length of an ARCnet coaxial network is six kilometers.

Another advantage of ARCnet is that the coaxial cable (RG62) is the same type used to connect IBM 3270 terminals to mainframes and is already in place in some buildings. ARCnet also supports fiber-optic and twisted-pair cables.

ARCnet is known for rock solid stability. The combination of star topology, mechanically and electrically stable coaxial cable, and the token-passing protocol gained ARCnet a reputation for reliability. It is no accident that there are few troubleshooting tools for ARCnet; specialized tools are not required in the rare event that something goes wrong with an ARCnet network.

LAN Cabling

Every network needs cabling to physically connect the computers. Cabling must be compatible with the topology and network protocol. Most networks use shielded or unshielded twisted-pair cabling, coaxial cabling, or fiber-optic cabling. Some networks are wireless or have wireless components.

Twisted-Pair Cable

Twisted-pair cabling is available either unshielded or shielded. **Unshielded twisted-pair (UTP) cable** usually combines four pairs of wires inside a jacket. Each pair has a different number of twists per inch. The twisting helps cancel interference from adjacent pairs (crosstalk) or other external sources, such as EMI. UTP looks like telephone wire but transmits data, not voice. RJ-45 connectors, which are slightly larger than regular telephone wire connectors (RJ-11), are used with UTP. UTP supports data transfer rates from 1 MB per second to 100 MB per second and is the least expensive type of cable.

Shielded twisted-pair (STP) cable has a foil wrapping around the pairs of wire and may have a woven copper braid wrapped around the entire assembly. This wrapping provides a higher degree of protection from EMI. STP cable is more expensive than UTP.

Coaxial Cable

Coaxial cable, also called **coax**, consists of a single copper wire surrounded by insulation, wrapped with braided copper to shield it from outside electrical signals and internal signal radiation. The assembly is covered with a plastic sleeve. The braided copper shielding acts as a second wire and a grounding connection. The connector used with coax is called a **British Naval Connector,** or a **BNC** connector. Coaxial cable is more expensive than twisted-pair cable but is commonly used in Ethernet networks.

10Base5 uses RG8 or RG11 coax cable, commonly called **thicknet** (the cable is about 0.5 inches thick). Connections to the thicknet cable are made with a **vampire tap**. The vampire tap and installation tools pierce the cable and make a connection without cutting the cable into separate pieces. The thicknet cable can be tapped while in operation. An electronic signal-conditioning device called a **transceiver** connects between the tap and computer. A DB15 cable connects the transceiver to the computer network card **attachment unit interface (AUI)** port. The physical ends of each cable segment must have 50-ohm terminators installed. As many as 100 transceivers can be connected to a 10Base5 cable segment.

10Base2 uses RG58 coax cable, commonly called **thinnet** (the cable is about 0.25 inches thick). Thinnet cable is physically easier to handle than thicknet. Stations are connected to the cable using a BNC T connector. Adding BNC connectors to a thinnet cable requires cutting the coax cable. Transceivers are integrated on the network adapter card. The first and last T-connectors in the network cabling must have 50-ohm terminators on one end. As many as 30 transceivers can be connected to a 10Base2 backbone.

10BaseT hubs or concentrators are frequently connected to a coaxial backbone cable. Though hubs can have 64 PCs attached, they count as only one transceiver on the coaxial cable.

Fiber-Optic Cable

Fiber-optic cable carries pulses of laser light over a thin strand of glass or plastic optical conductor. A thicker glass material, known as **cladding**, surrounds the thin inner glass fiber. The cladding refracts light back into the core. An external plastic covering protects each fiber. Multiple fibers are assembled into cables and protected by a tough outer material that varies, depending on the cable design and intended use.

Several materials are used to protect fiber bundles inside the outer covering. Tight configuration fiber-optic cable uses a layer of fiberglass, metallic wires, or Kevlar strands to surround the fiber bundle, adding tensile strength to the cable assembly. Tight configuration fiber-optic cable is used inside buildings. Loose configuration fiber-optic cable is filled with a liquid or gel to repel water. All plastics are porous to liquids, and fiber-optic strands are degraded by contact with water, so the gel prevents any liquids that penetrate the outer cable material from coming in contact with the glass fibers. The gel is toxic and flammable. Loose configuration fiber-optic cables are used outside of buildings.

Proper handling of fiber-optic cable is critical. Bending the cable so that it exceeds the minimum bend radius (tighter than specified by the manufacturer) can break some or all of the enclosed fibers. Glass fibers have very little tensile strength. Pulling on a fiber can cause it to break somewhere along its length, usually rendering the cable useless.

The diameter of fiber-optic cable is also important. The most popular multi-mode fiber size is a 62.5-micron core with a 125-micron cladding. The core of multi-mode fiber is large enough to allow multiple light paths. The transmitted light reflects and bounces its way down the cable. Multi-mode fiber is easily aligned with mass produced low power laser diodes and can reach tens of kilometers in length.

Splicing fiber-optic cable or adding connectors to the cable ends is a tedious and time consuming task. Installing and testing connectors can be a significant part of the installation cost of fiber-optic cable.

The most popular single-mode fiber size is a 8.3-micron core with 125-micron cladding. The core of single-mode fiber is just large enough to allow a single pathway for light. Single-mode fiber is used with high power laser transmitters and can reach for hundreds of kilometers. Single-mode fiber-optic cable is significantly more expensive to produce and purchase than multi-mode fiber.

Infrared light is not visible to the human eye. You cannot determine whether a fiber-optic cable is carrying data by looking into it. Using a magnifying glass to examine the end of a fiber-optic cable that is live can cause permanent eye damage! Fiber-optic cable installers use a special microscope to examine the fiber ends. A built-in infrared filter prevents accidental eye injuries from laser light.

Fiber-optic cable does not emit and is immune to external EMI. It is the best choice in areas where high EMI levels exist. Because glass is not electrically conductive, fiber is used in hazardous environments, where even a spark would be dangerous. Fiber-optic cable should be used anywhere a network cable leaves one building and enters another. This prevents nearby lightning strikes from being conducted into either building to damage or destroy attached computers, hubs, or repeaters. In addition, tapping or eavesdropping on a fiber-optic cable is extremely difficult. Cutting or connecting to a fiber-optic cable changes the light loss and is, therefore, detectable. Fiber-optic cable is a good choice for high security networks.

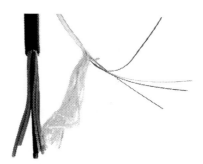

Fiber-Optic Cable

Wireless Networking

Wireless networks use infrared light, radio frequencies, or microwave signals.

- **Infrared light** from low power LEDs to high power lasers connect users in a small area to line of sight locations. Bright light, dust, fog, or opaque materials interfere with light-based wireless connections.

- **Radio frequency connections** can be low power units with restricted ranges or high power long distance connections that reach around the globe. Radio frequencies are susceptible to eavesdropping and EMI, but encryption techniques minimize the possibility of eavesdropping.

- **Microwave connections** can be land- or space-based. Land-based microwave systems use narrow or wide focus beams to connect line of sight locations. Space-based systems allow global transmission of data to and from any place with a clear view of the sky. Aircraft, marine, or land-based transmitters can use space-based microwave systems. Connection of remote sites using satellite microwave transmission can be less expensive than running a physical cable.

Interconnectivity

Organizations use service providers to distribute information via a network to different locations within the information system. For example, local and long distance telephone services are used to route data to locations where it is not feasible for an organization to run its own cabling.

Organizations and service providers also use specific hardware devices to distribute information, either locally or across long distances. These devices are called repeaters, bridges, routers, brouters, and gateways.

Repeaters *— connect 2 lan site together to extend the distance*

As an electrical signal is transmitted over cable, its strength decreases. A **repeater** is a device that regenerates cable signals to expand the network. Repeaters often are used to connect workstations in remote parts of a working environment, such as connecting a warehouse to the front office.

Bridges *_slow*

Local bridges connect LANs, usually within the same building. **Remote bridges** have ports for analog or digital telecommunication links to other locations.

A **bridge** is a device that connects two similar LANs. A bridge allows a workstation on one cable segment to send messages to workstations on another cable segment, without creating a new logical network. A bridge also can be used to isolate traffic between two cable segments, reducing the amount of

example token ring to token ring

traffic on each segment and improving performance. Some bridges can link only networks using the same protocol; however, **heterogeneous** bridges can translate between protocols.

Routers _ slow

A **router** is a device that routes messages from one network to another. It is used to internetwork similar or dissimilar networks. The router selects the most expedient route based on traffic load, line speeds, costs or metrics, and network failures. Routers are similar to bridges but can handle multiple protocols, multiple addresses, and multiple network segments.

 The Internet can be described as a large number of interconnected routers.

Brouters

A **brouter** combines the features of a bridge and a router. For instance, a brouter can be programmed to route protocols that can be routed, and to bridge protocols that cannot be routed.

Gateways

A **gateway** is a device that acts as a translator between two systems that do not use the same protocol. Because gateways translate protocols, their performance is typically slower than bridges or routers.

mail

Review

Local area networks (LANs) are used to share resources, including devices and data. Peer-to-peer networks are used when security issues are limited and only a few PCs are involved. Client/server networks use a dedicated machine to control data access, manage the network, and store programs and data.

LAN **topologies** include **bus, star**, and **ring**. Variations and combinations of these exist.

Protocols determine how networked computers communicate. Common protocols are **Ethernet, Token Ring**, and **ARCnet**.

LAN cabling includes **shielded** and **unshielded twisted-pair, coaxial**, and **fiber-optic**. Each type has advantages and disadvantages relating to reliability, the length of cable that can be used, and cost. Wireless networks connect devices without using cable.

Hardware devices used to transmit data include repeaters, bridges, routers, brouters, and gateways.

LESSON 12: TROUBLESHOOTING

After completing this lesson, you will be able to:

+ set up PCs in a proper environment

+ verify errors in the power-on self test

+ use an organized process to troubleshoot hardware and software problems

+ troubleshoot PC components and peripheral devices

+ set system interrupts

Providing the Proper Environment

Computers are expensive pieces of equipment that require moderate temperatures and a clean area to operate reliably. Personal computers operate well in most office environments.

When selecting a location for a PC, do the following:

* Use a large, sturdy, flat surface that will support the weight of the computer and peripherals.

* Provide adequate air circulation. Avoid blocking the air intake area of the front grill or the air exhaust area in the back of the computer. Also, be careful not to block the ventilation area on the top of monitors. Monitors are cooled by convection only, so blocking the exhaust ventilation area on a monitor will cause it to overheat and fail prematurely.

 A stack of papers on top of a monitor makes a good fuel source for a nasty office fire.

* Choose a cool, dry location with no direct sunlight. All electronic devices operate better and longer at lower temperatures. Optimally, PCs should be operated in an ambient temperature range of 60° to 75° F. Temperatures above 80° F place added stress on computer electronics. The internal temperature of components ranges from 15° to more than 30° higher than room temperature. High temperature alarms are available to indicate when the internal computer temperature exceeds a safe level.

PCs should be located away from sources of liquids and where humidity is controlled. Spills, drips, or rising water will permanently damage floppy and hard disk drives. If the PC is operating when exposed to a liquid, various components can short out. High humidity is rarely a problem, and can actually be beneficial because it decreases levels of static electricity in the area. However, condensing humidity can damage computer boards as well as hard drives. Condensation occurs when a warm computer is turned off and cools in a humid environment. If computers must be operated in a humid environment, it is better to leave them running continuously to avoid internal condensation. In extreme situations, sealed cases are available to allow operation in severe environmental and industrial areas.

Exposure to sunlight will cause overheating inside the PC or monitor case and damage to plastics commonly used in computer and peripheral cases.

◆ Limit dust and smoke particles. The fan in a PC is very efficient at pulling office dust into the computer case. Dust settles on computer components, providing an insulating layer. A dusty computer will overheat and fail even in an otherwise adequate office environment. Periodic cleaning of the computer by blowing excess dust out of the case is very good preventive maintenance.

Industrial areas where fine dust particles are present create a specific problem for PCs. Industrial dust is often electrically conductive and can short out electrical components on the motherboard. Iron oxide and carbon dust particles are small enough to infiltrate the pressure equalization air filters of hard drives. If dust enters a hard drive, it will cause a head crash.

Tobacco smoke is very hazardous to computers. Because the smoke contains tars, it will coat all the exposed surfaces of the PC with a sticky acidic layer. Dust that settles on the tar coating cannot be removed by blowing it away. The acidic nature of the tar substance also causes motherboard corrosion. Intermittent connections between the data bus and expansion cards are common in computers used around smokers. A spray solvent may clean connectors and circuit boards enough to return them to operation. Generally, motherboards that have failed in a computer contaminated with tobacco tar should be replaced.

- Ensure that the power supply is properly grounded and that the polarity is correct. Test the AC outlet for a proper ground and correct polarity using a circuit tester or multimeter.

 Remember, a reverse wired power outlet presents a shock hazard to the computer user and can damage or destroy the computer.

- Use a surge suppresser to protect computer circuitry. The best surge suppressor is far less expensive than the lowest priced computer. A surge suppressor must have a good earth ground to stop surges. Many better surge suppressors also monitor the AC outlet for improper wiring.

- Identify magnetic fields that can erase data on floppy disks and distort video displays. Move telephones and stereo speakers as far away from data as possible. Use only speakers that are magnetically shielded to minimize problems with the monitor and magnetic media. Store diskettes and backup tapes away from the monitor, because monitors use magnetic fields to write to the display screen.

 Avoid using magnets in the area around a computer. Frequently, paper holder stands use a magnet to hold papers. This small magnet is more than powerful enough to erase diskettes that are accidentally laid against them.

Power-On Self Test (POST)

most of the time memory or monitor

When you turn on a computer, it performs a **power-on self test (POST)**. Instructions for the POST reside in the ROM BIOS. If the POST fails before video display is available, it will issue a series of long and short beeps. By referring to the manufacturer's table of beep codes, a technician can determine what step of the POST failed. Beep codes are not standard; they vary among BIOS and motherboard manufacturers. The POST performs the following tests:

- The program counter in the CPU is reset to location F000; F000 is the starting location for the POST in ROM BIOS.

- The registers and flags of the CPU are tested by generating a checksum that is verified against a value contained in ROM. If the values do not agree, the system halts.

- The DMA controller is tested for proper function. If the DMA controller malfunctions, the system halts.

- The interrupt controller is tested for proper function. If this test fails, the system sounds a long beep and a short beep and then halts.

- The speed of the timer is tested. If the timer is defective, the system sounds a long beep and a short beep and then halts.

- Expansion slots and serial and parallel ports are tested.

- If ROM Basic is available, POST calculates a checksum and verifies it against a value stored in the Basic ROM chip set.

- The video card is tested. If it malfunctions, the system sounds one long beep and two short beeps. If no problems exist, the Video BIOS is copied into the upper memory blocks of RAM, if video shadowing is supported and enabled in the system setup.

- The read/write capabilities of RAM are tested by writing a byte of data and reading it to compare the results. If they differ, a memory error occurs.

- The keyboard and its interface are tested to verify that they are connected and that a key is not stuck. Pressing a key during the test phase can incorrectly report a keyboard failure. A keyboard error message is displayed if the test fails.

- The disk drives and their controllers are tested. If the information sent back to the CPU does not match that in CMOS, the system sounds a short beep and displays an error message.

- Disk drives are reset and motors are activated. If a problem occurs, a 601 class error message displays, and the system sounds a short beep. On older systems with Basic available in ROM, DOS is loaded into memory.

- The remaining adapter cards are tested, and if found, their BIOS is copied into RAM. POST issues a short beep and loads the boot record, which then controls the computer. The beep at the completion of POST is normal and indicates the successful completion of all tests.

The Problem-Solving Process

To become an accomplished technician, you must develop a strategy for solving problems. Together with the appropriate level of knowledge and experience, this strategy will make you an effective and efficient troubleshooter. The problem-solving process is described by the following five steps:

1. Gather data to define the problem clearly.

2. Develop a plan.

3. Execute the plan.

4. Document the process.

5. Monitor the results.

Step 1: Gather Data

Before investing a lot of time troubleshooting a problem, eliminate the possibility of user error. The results of a user operation may be different than what the user expected, but this doesn't guarantee a problem with the computer or network.

When a problem is reported, you should determine that the user performed the procedure correctly. For instance, if a printer prints strange characters, is the wrong printer driver selected? If document text suddenly disappears, did the user select cut instead of copy? If the user cannot run the network database program, is he or she logged onto the network?

Next, consider the possibility that the procedure worked properly, but the user does not realize it. For example, if the user selected a network printer that is located in another room but expected the print job to come out on a local printer, the operation was successful but not what the user expected. By carefully eliminating the possibility of user error, valuable time will not be wasted troubleshooting a nonexistent problem.

If a verifiable problem does exist, gather more information by performing the following preliminary steps:

- If the computer will boot, run a virus scan on all hard drives. If a virus is found, remove it and restart your investigation. It is possible that the virus had nothing to do with the reported symptoms.

- Check the hardware. Are all cables present and securely connected? Check cables, especially VGA monitor cables, for bent or damaged pins. If the cable is not keyed, is pin 1 connected to pin 1 on each end?

- If the hard drive is involved, determine when the last backup was performed, or back up the hard drive before continuing.

- Turn off the computer and all external peripheral devices. Leave the power off for 15 to 30 seconds, then turn everything back on again.

- If the computer operates on a network, suspect a security access problem. Determine whether a more privileged user or a different user account will run the failing software.

- Ensure that current versions of all software and device drivers are installed. Don't troubleshoot a problem that a software manufacturer solved six months ago.

Experienced troubleshooters frequently find and correct failures without systematically solving the problem. This is called a quick fix. One component or configuration may always cause the same problem. After seeing the same symptoms and systematically troubleshooting to the same conclusion several times, the technician should know the correct solution without using a step-by-step method. For instance, hearts, smiley faces, or line drawing symbols printed on the top of each page of a print job indicates a printer driver mismatch.

If the preceding steps do not solve the problem, consider all the symptoms. If the symptoms appear to implicate both hardware and software, troubleshoot the hardware problem first. Troubleshooting software is useful only after you are satisfied that the hardware is functioning properly. Also remember that several problems can occur at the same time. Solve the most severe problem first, and then resolve minor problems, because the first problem could be causing others.

Try to verify all reported symptoms. If a symptom cannot be reproduced, you will not know when you have corrected the problem. Unverifiable symptoms can be the result of intermittent failures or an error on the part of the user. It is common for users to describe problems in terms of what they think the solution is. A report of a broken hard drive might mean anything from a head crash to a lost file. In order to separate a user's opinion from a problem symptom, ask the user very specific questions such as "What is the exact error message you received?" This information is more useful than a verbal report of a failed hard drive. For example, if the error message is "File Not Found," you know the problem is not a head crash. Always ask the user to demonstrate the problem and find out when the problem started.

Next, determine what if anything has been changed recently. Electronic devices are prone to failure soon after being installed. This is known as an **infant failure**. Look for newly installed or unauthorized software. New versions of software can have problems, can cause other software to stop working, or can be improperly configured. Utilities, games, and screen savers installed by users can compromise the computer's operation.

Look for external conditions that occur when the problem is noticed. Does a computer lock up or reboot at 4:30 every afternoon? Does the UPS battery backup alarm go off between 2 and 3 pm on sunny days, but not on overcast days? Does the network connection fail every day between 5 and 6 pm? Does the computer lockup or reboot only when operated by one person? Look for patterns in the symptoms, especially with intermittent or difficult to diagnose problems.

Sometimes a failure is so critical that time is not available for systematic troubleshooting. If a critical file server fails, it might be better to move the hard drive to a similar computer and get the system running again. Later, you can systematically troubleshoot the failed computer to find the problem.

Sometimes error messages mean only that a problem exists, but do not accurately identify the problem. A RAM error can cause a "mouse buffer overflow" message. A printer "out of paper" message indicate a paper jam. Error messages can be completely misleading. Always investigate the indicated problem, but understand that the error message may have nothing to do with the failure.

Step 2: Develop a Plan

Based on the information you gathered in the first step, decide whether user error, hardware, operating system software, or an application software program would be the most likely to cause the problem. Develop two or three alternative solutions. Prioritize these possibilities on the likelihood of the solution being correct and on the cost of implementing the solution. The cost of a solution could include parts costs, technician's labor costs, or the cost of the system being down. For instance, if no video display appears on the monitor, possible alternatives would include a bad monitor, a failed video card, an unplugged or damaged monitor cable, a failed motherboard, bad system RAM, or a failed power supply. Because checking the monitor for a power indication and good video cable connection is easiest, that should be done before you open the computer case. Testing the monitor has a lower cost in time and a higher probability of correcting the problem than replacing the video card or motherboard.

Step 3: Execute the Plan

Divide the problem into the smallest reasonably testable steps. Check each step by changing one item at a time. If you change multiple components or configurations at one time, you cannot know which action fixed the problem. After making one change, check the system to see if the problem is solved or the symptom has changed. For instance, if changing a SIMM module corrects a "Memory Test Error" message, but when the computer boots it gives a "Bad or Missing Command Interpreter" error message, two different and possibly unrelated problems exist. Changing the memory module corrected the first failure, which was hiding the second failure.

Step 4: Document the Process

Detailed documentation of the troubleshooting process and the resultant solution can save you time and effort in future troubleshooting endeavors.

Always record the symptoms of the problem and the solution that finally corrected it. The best troubleshooting aid is a good history of previous repairs. A good service history also is a rich source of training information for new technicians. They can gain troubleshooting experience quickly by reviewing the symptoms and solutions to problems previously corrected. New technicians also benefit from seeing the methodology of more experienced technicians.

 A good service history also will highlight a pattern of failures that may not be obvious otherwise. If computers in one area are failing frequently with common problems, some other solution may be needed. For example, if items that generate a lot of heat, such as hard drives or processors, are failing faster than normal, additional cooling could help. If a particular part fails frequently, a better replacement may be needed, or a larger stock of spare parts may be required. Something as simple as more frequent cleaning can solve high failure rates of some parts.

Step 5: Monitor the Results

Ask the user to try operations that previously failed. Be sure the problem is completely resolved before ending the service call. Problems you found and corrected could have masked other problems, which will be discovered soon after the user starts using the computer again.

Failure of some parts can damage other components, which will fail in the near future. For instance, a power supply failure can cause a momentary overvoltage before the internal fuse blows. Hard drives or motherboard components can be damaged but still function for a short time. Caution the user to watch for additional failures and to be conscientious about data backups.

If additional failures occur, good documentation of the computer's service history will be extremely helpful.

 Regular data backups are important following any discovery of failed hardware.

Diagnostic Tools

The best diagnostic tool is the five senses of an experienced technician. Does anything look damaged? Do any components look burned or discolored? Are all socketed ICs fully seated in their sockets? Is there a burned smell? Are unusual sounds heard when the computer operates? Do drives sound too loud, or are they not making any sound? Are hard drives too hot? You can use four of your five senses, sight, smell, hearing, and touch, to detect a problem and save yourself hours of troubleshooting.

Diagnostic software is the next most important tool. Different operating systems provide some diagnostic software such as CHKDSK, SCANDISK, MSD, and the System icon in Windows 95 and Windows NT. If diagnostics provided with the operating system are appropriate, they are available on most computers.

Third party diagnostics manufacturers generally produce programs with much greater capabilities and range of tests than operating system supplied utilities. Several different diagnostic products might be needed to address the range of problems a technician regularly faces.

Many times, diagnostic software includes wrap plugs. Serial and parallel ports must have diagnostic wrap plugs installed to completely test each port. Wrap plugs are not generic. Diagnostic software usually requires the wrap plug to be wired a specific way. Often, the documentation that accompanies this software will illustrate how to fabricate additional wrap plugs.

A standard telephone is very useful for troubleshooting modem problems. If a standard consumer telephone will not work when plugged into a modem wall jack, the modem will not either.

Special purpose hardware diagnostic cards called POST cards are sometimes useful for troubleshooting motherboard and interrupt problems. High end POST cards contain their own processor and memory. They can test and isolate a motherboard failure, even if the motherboard cannot be booted. Low end POST cards indicate the error condition discovered during the power-on self test with much greater accuracy than beep codes or error messages.

Troubleshooting Computer Components

This section lists troubleshooting issues and possible solutions related to computer components.

Motherboard

Individual motherboard components and expansion slots can fail.

Lack of video display and a beep code during the boot process implicate the motherboard. Try to test the motherboard by unplugging all expansion boards and power cables to all drives. Change the video card and memory if you still receive only a beep code. Test the motherboard on the test bench after removing it from the computer case. Shorts beneath the motherboard, between a circuit and a metal spacer (stand off), can cause the motherboard to fail the POST.

Press down any ICs mounted in sockets. Repeated heating and cooling cycles from daily turning on and off of the computer can cause ICs to slowly loosen in their sockets. This is known as **chip creep**.

If the motherboard will not complete a POST after being reduced to its simplest configuration, replacing the motherboard is probably the best solution.

If your system has fatal errors and you do not get a video display, you have fatal POST errors. Problems that can cause fatal POST errors include:

- Loss of a video card
- No RAM or bad RAM
- No keyboard

Memory

Memory is checked by the POST. Intermittent memory or parity errors are called **soft errors**. A consistent memory error that reports the same error location every time a memory test runs is a **hard failure** and indicates a failed chip.

Some memory performs a continuous self-check of data integrity called a parity check. Many new memory modules do not use parity. If the motherboard setup is configured for parity memory, a non parity memory module will fail the parity test. Be sure the parity test option is set correctly for the memory modules in use.

Memory error codes specify the location of the failed chip and bank, but the error codes may or may not be useful in finding the failed memory module. Software diagnostics programs are more useful in isolating a soft memory failure. Load memory diagnostics software and configure it for continuous testing. Swapping a known good memory module until the bad module is found helps isolate hard memory failures. If a contact problem exists between the memory module and socket, removing and reinstalling the module can correct the error. Be sure to clean the socket and the module to prevent return of intermittent problems.

Power Supplies

 Do not attempt to repair a power supply yourself, because power supplies contain capacitors, which hold an electrical charge for an extended period of time.

You can use a voltmeter to check for appropriate output DC voltages and determine whether the power supply is working properly. Remember that power supplies require a load on the output to operate.

If a power supply malfunctions, replacement is normally the most cost-effective action.

Power supplies convert 120 VAC to +5, -5, +12, and -12 VDC. If you suspect that your power supply is not functioning properly, check the +5 VDC lead first.

If a new power supply will not work properly, check the input voltage switch. Most power supplies are set to accept 120 or 220 VAC. If the selector switch is set for 220 VAC, the power supply will not run on 120 VAC.

Disk Drives

If hard drive errors occur, evaluate the value of the data contained on the drive before attempting to correct the problem. If a recent backup of the drive is available, and the loss of information saved since the backup is acceptable, various techniques and third-party software programs are available that can successfully correct hard drive errors. If the data is valuable and replacing it would not be cost-effective, do not attempt to repair the drive. Restore the latest backup to a different hard drive. If the restored data is acceptable, continue to repair the failed drive. If the restoration fails, or more data is lost than is acceptable, sending the failed drive to a third party data recovery specialty company is the remaining choice. Data recovery companies are expensive, but could be a bargain compared to losing important data.

Attempts to recover data or repair a failed drive can corrupt remaining data and prevent a data recovery company from saving anything. If you think a data recovery service may be needed, do not attempt to repair the drive.

If a newly installed drive does not work, verify that the ribbon cable is properly installed at the drive and the controller. Reversing pin 1 on the ribbon cable from the controller to the drive will prevent some hard drives from spinning. Incorrect cable connections also can prevent the motherboard from booting.

Verify or set the jumpers on IDE devices. Two drives may be connected to one cable. One of the drives must be set to be the Master; the other must be set to be the Slave. Some drives use a third designation of Only Drive. IDE hard drives are typically shipped from the factory jumpered in the Master or Only Drive configuration. Tape drives and CD-ROMs may also be connected to the cable along with hard drives. They typically are shipped jumpered in the slave configuration. Connecting a slow IDE device like a CD-ROM drive on the same cable with a fast hard drive slows the drive access speed to match the CD-ROM. Some hard drives support different speeds of operation by devices on the same cable.

Most SCSI drives are low level formatted by the manufacturer. Reformatting a SCSI drive at low level does not cause problems but is rarely necessary. The most common error in configuring a SCSI device is providing proper bus termination. Remember, two and only two terminations can be present on a SCSI bus. Only the devices on the physical ends of the SCSI cable can provide termination.

The strength of magnetic data is decreased every time the drive read-write head passes over it. Data files can be rewritten many times, which renews their magnetic energy. Program files are usually written to the drive only when originally installed. If a read error occurs with a program file, reinstalling the program could be sufficient to restore the program readability. However, the data written to define sector and track boundaries is written only when the hard drive is originally low level formatted by the manufacturer or installing technician. If track or sector data becomes too weak to read, data contained in the area cannot be accessed. A **Sector not found** error indicates a problem reading track or sector information. Rewriting the low level format information can correct the problem; however, a low level format will destroy all data on the hard drive.

Early hard drives that used magnetic oxide coatings suffered from a phenomenon known as track creep. If data representing a binary 1 was written adjacent to another 1, the magnetic areas would tend to move away from each other. Write precompensation attempted to correct this drift. Low level formatting the drive repositions the tracks and sectors. The change to thinner plated or sputtered magnetic media eliminated this problem.

IDE drives have servo alignment tracks that help locate tracks accurately. Only the drive manufacturer can write the servo track. Older diagnostic programs will overwrite the servo track, which could disable the drive. Losing the servo track will at least lower the reliability of an IDE drive. Current diagnostic software that has an IDE low level format option is programmed to step over the servo track and will not overwrite it.

Hard drive diagnostics sometimes corrects software related drive problems that operating system utilities cannot. Some utilities are intended to be used for routine maintenance also. They may make a copy of critical file tables and hide it on the drive. If the drive tables are corrupted, an old copy saved by the utility may recover most data.

Accidentally formatting a hard drive is still a common user error. If a hard drive format is started, do not interrupt the process. After the drive has finished the format process, run an operating system or diagnostic utility unformat program. Unformatting a hard drive is more likely to be successful if no new data has been written to the drive after being accidentally formatted.

- **Lost clusters** are a common hard drive problem. Run ScanDisk from MS-DOS or Windows 95. Run CHKDSK /F from the command prompt to repair lost clusters using Windows NT. A filename will be assigned to each lost cluster. Delete these files to free disk space. Lost clusters usually do not indicate lost or corrupt data. Trying to recover data in lost clusters is normally not useful.

- **Cross-linked files** indicate a serious hard drive error. When ScanDisk or CHKDSK reports cross-linked files, note the filenames and delete both cross-linked files. Restore the corrupted files from a recent backup. Reoccurrence of cross-linked files indicate a failing hard drive, a virus, or a user that is turning off the computer without exiting programs properly.

- **Master boot record** errors are usually noticed when the hard drive fails to boot. If the boot area of the hard drive is corrupted, the master boot record may be rewritten using an undocumented MS DOS FDISK option FDISK/MBR. Third party disk diagnostic utilities also can repair master boot record errors. If the track 0 area contains an unrecoverable error, try low level formatting the hard drive. A low level format will destroy any data on the drive. Track 0 errors frequently cannot be repaired. Replacing the drive and restoring the latest backup may be the only choice.

- **Viruses** can attack the master boot record, file allocation table, partition table, or executable files. Hard drive errors are frequently a symptom of a virus activation. Depending on the design of the virus, it could spread to other disks by infecting a diskette or attaching to a file stored on a file server. When activated, the virus could corrupt or delete files or tables.

Be sure all diagnostics diskettes are write-protected. Always scan each computer before servicing it (to be sure a virus is not causing the problem) and after service is completed (to be sure you did not leave a new virus). Careless technicians can spread viruses to every computer they service.

If a virus is found, caution the user that any diskette they have (including any at home and their home computer hard drive) may be infected. Using an infected diskette will instantly reinfect the hard drive. Recommend a systematic scanning of all diskettes using a good anti-virus program.

Controllers and Adapters

Expansion bus cards are keyed and will fit into only the correct bus slot. Expansion cards should fit securely into the data bus connector sockets. Cards that do not fully seat in the sockets will make poor contact and can be dislodged easily. It is not unusual for expansion cards to come out of their sockets usually after the computer is moved. Expansion cards should be secured by tightening the screw that holds their mounting brackets to the case. Some cards obtain electrical ground through the metal bracket. Such cards will operate intermittently if a securing screw is not used. If the metal bracket does not sit down flush with the case ledge, do not force it into place by screwing the metal bracket down. Forcing the card bracket into place transfers tremendous downward force to the motherboard. A motherboard bowed by the force of an expansion card can fail quickly.

If the data bus socket or the expansion card edge connectors become dirty or contaminated, clean them with commercial solvents made for cleaning electrical contacts. Never use an abrasive cleaner like a pencil eraser. Most electrical contacts are gold, tin, or bronze plated copper. Plating protects the copper from corrosion and normal oxidation. If poor cleaning techniques remove the plating, the connection will oxidize very quickly. Replacing the damaged board is the only reasonable alternative. Removing, cleaning, and reinstalling expansion boards often will correct intermittent contact problems.

If an expansion board uses a cable, be careful to connect pin 1 of the cable to pin 1 of the board connector. If you cannot determine where pin 1 should be, refer to the expansion board documentation or contact the manufacturer. Do not guess at the correct position because damage to the expansion board or the plugged-in device could result.

SCSI II host adapters have a DB25 female connector for the external cable port. The printer port also uses a DB25 female connector. If a printer cable is plugged into a SCSI II port, the interior SCSI cable will melt, and the SCSI interface will be destroyed. Consider plugging an empty DB25 male connector into the external port to avoid this mistake.

All expansion boards must have IRQ, DMA, and I/O memory addresses. Some boards use only two of the three settings, and other boards use multiple settings. Documenting the resources in use will minimize future installation problems. Windows 95 and Windows NT provide a useful self-documentation feature, accessible through the System icon. It is possible to print a report of all resources currently in use. Even with advanced software or hardware diagnostic tools, it is easier to document and correctly install new expansion boards than it is to troubleshoot resource conflicts.

Monitors

 Because of high voltages and other hazards, do not attempt to repair a monitor. Take it to an authorized service center.

It is unusual for a PC technician to repair monitors. Specialized training, expensive test equipment, and technical documentation supplied by the manufacturer are required to repair any monitor. Never remove the back cover of a monitor. Internal monitor power supplies store voltages in excess of 15,000 volts, even after being turned off for months.

Monitors contain capacitors that hold electrical charges. Accidental contact with these charges can cause severe injuries or death.

Monitors also contain cathode ray tubes (CRTs), which contain a vacuum. If you drop a CRT and it breaks, the vacuum implosion can scatter broken glass everywhere, causing severe cuts.

Some monitors have removable cables and power cords. Be sure the power cord is securely attached. Some power cords are very tight. They can appear to be connected, but the power cord is not fully seated. If in doubt, unplug and reconnect the power cord.

High density DB15 connectors used for VGA monitors are very fragile. Their thin pins are easily bent or pushed back into the socket if pins are misaligned when the plug is connected. If no video displays, or one color is missing, carefully check the pins of the video cable under a strong light. Bent pins can be realigned with needle-nosed pliers, but they can be broken easily. The VGA cable can be replaced by a monitor service center, if the cable is permanently attached to the monitor.

Monitor failures are easily diagnosed by moving the suspect monitor to another computer, or plugging a known good monitor into the computer.

Nearby EMI fields will cause a monitor to display slow or fast waves that move vertically across the screen. Moving the monitor should correct the problem.

Monitor screens can become magnetized by unshielded speakers or nearby transformers. The black brick style power adapters used by modems, digitizing tablets, tape drives, and other external peripherals can cause EMI distortion and may magnetize the monitor screen. A magnetized screen will display a color distortion (usually dark red, blue, or purple) in one area. Some monitors have a manual degauss button to correct the problem. Other monitors automatically degauss when turned on. Do not cycle the monitor on and off to attempt to degauss the screen. The distortion should go away within a few weeks. If the screen remains distorted, a monitor repair technician can degauss the screen with a monitor demagnetizer tool, or degausser.

Monitor screens attract dust because of their electrostatic charge. Clean monitor screens and the case with a soft cloth sprayed with a window cleaner. *Never spray liquids on the monitor screen or case.*

Keyboards

Exchange a failed keyboard with a known good unit. If the new keyboard works, connect the old keyboard to a different computer. If the suspect keyboard still does not work, it should be replaced.

Some keyboards are hard to connect. Be sure the connector is fully seated in the keyboard socket. If a miniature DIN connector is used, be sure the keyboard is plugged into the correct socket. The keyboard connector will fit into the mouse port connector, but the keyboard will not operate.

Because the keyboard and mouse receive power through their cables, disconnect and connect these cables only when the computer power is turned off.

Keyboards contain active electronics that can fail, but the motherboard contains the keyboard controller. If the controller fails, the motherboard might have to be replaced.

Keyboards are vulnerable to physical damage, contamination, and mechanical wear. Keep liquids away from keyboards. If liquid is spilled onto a keyboard, shut down the computer as quickly as possible. Due to the low cost, contaminated keyboards are usually replaced. Periodic cleaning by blowing air into the key area while holding the keyboard upside down will remove various staples, paper clips, pins, and other foreign materials that keyboards collect. Clean the keys by wiping with a soft cloth moistened with a window cleaner. Do not spray liquid cleaners onto a keyboard.

You can use a voltmeter to check the keyboard DIN connector on a PC. Place one lead of the meter on the ground socket and check remaining sockets for DC voltage. Readings should be between 2.5 and 5 volts.

The following table can help you locate the ground socket on your computer:

Connector	Socket	Function
Larger DIN	1	keyboard clock signal
	2	data signal
	3	keyboard reset signal
	4	ground
	5	VDC power supply
PS/2 Mini-DIN	1	keyboard data
	2	not used
	3	ground
	4	+5 VDC
	5	keyboard clock signal
	6	not used

Modems

Many modem manufacturers provide diagnostic test software. Third-party diagnostic software also runs many detailed tests on modems.

Internal modems have their own UART installed and must be assigned unique IRQ and I/O addresses. Often the selection of these resources on the internal modem conflicts with the computer's preinstalled COM ports. Modems configured to conflict with other devices in the computer usually do not work; however, they can work for a while or intermittently.

Internal modems normally are assigned to COM2, or COM1 after the installed COM2 or COM1 is disabled. Failing to disable the installed COM port will guarantee a conflict.

You can manually test a modem using AT and &Tx commands. You can perform self tests on PC communications ports, because they are bi-directional; the message that the port receives can originate from the port itself.

The following table summarizes these self tests:

Command	Test Performed
&T0	End Test
&T1	Analog Loopback (AL)
&T2	Reserved
&T3	Local Digital Loopback (LDL)
&T4	Grant Remote Digital Loopback (RDL)
&T5	Deny RDL (default setting)
&T6	Initiate RDL testing
&T7	Initiate RDL with self-test and error detection
&T8	Initiate AL with self-test and error detection

Ending Tests

To terminate a modem test, use one of the following commands:

- AT &T0

- AT S18=20 &T1 (places a 20-second timer on register S18)

- ATZ (resets the modem)

- ATHT (hangs up the phone)

- ++++++

Analog Loopback (AL) Test

This test is used to determine whether the transmitter and receiver on a local modem are working. While it is running, you type characters and they are echoed back to the screen. You initiate the test with the AT &M0 S18=20 &T1 command. The &M0 command puts the modem in normal mode, with error control disabled.

Analog Loopback Self Test

This is an AL test with error detection. The test sends a string of characters and tallies the number of errors. You initiate the test using the AT &T8 &T0 command, or use the AT S18 = 20 &T8 command for a timed test.

Local Digital Loopback (LDL) Test

This tests the remote modem and the telephone line between the modems. This test is performed at the site of the remote modem. From the modem at the remote site (A), you type a message, which is transmitted to the other modem (B), and then reflected to the remote modem (A).

To perform an LDL test, complete the following steps:

1. Issue the AT &M0 command to the local modem.

2. Establish a communication session between modems. Issue an ATDT phone number command to manually dial the remote modem.

3. When connected, issue the AT &T3 command to the local modem to start the LDL test.

4. Key in a short message from the remote modem. If the connection is good, the message will display on the remote terminal. Notify the other terminal that you are finished.

5. To end the test, issue the AT &T0 command.

6. Use the ATH0 command to hang up the telephone.

Remote Digital Loopback Test

This test checks both local and remote modems and the telephone line between them. It can be performed at either 1200 or 2400 bps. Both modems must be capable of ITU v.54bis data transmissions. You initiate the test with the AT &T6 &T0 or AT &T7 T0 command, or use the S18 command for a timed test.

Testing the Communications Port

If tests indicate that a modem is working properly, but communications are still not possible, the problem could be in the serial or RS 232 port. Connecting the modem to another serial port is the easiest way to determine whether a serial port is bad.

Testing a serial port requires special diagnostic equipment. You must use either a breakout box with indicator lights or a voltmeter and appropriate diagnostic software (PDIAGS.EXE for example). You can download PDIAGS.EXE from the Internet. Because a voltmeter usually is available, the following information is provided:

- Voltages over +3 VDC are used to send a 0, and voltages less than -3 VDC are used to send a 1.

- Voltages between -3 and +3 VDC are interpreted as neither 0 nor 1.

- You should read -3 VDC on pins 2 and 20 and +3 VDC on pin 4 of the port.

- Line 20 is the **data terminal ready (DTR)** line. **Data carrier detect (DCD)** can be tested by placing a jumper between pins 20 and 8. **Data set ready (DSR)** can be tested by placing a jumper between pins 20 and 6.

Universal Asynchronous Receiver/Transmitter (UART)

Serial ports contain UART chips. The UART can be an 8250, 16450, or 16550 chip. Upgrading to a 16550 chip is easy, because these chips usually are socketed. Serial cards also contain the 1488 and 1489 driver chips, which usually are soldered to the circuit board.

Serial Cable

If nothing is wrong with the port, the serial cable could be loose or broken. You can test the cable, or you can replace it. This test applies to external modems only, because internal modems do not require cabling.

Printers

Regardless of the type of printer, problems related to image creation, paper transport, and printer drivers can arise.

Dot-Matrix Printer Problems

Dot-matrix printers exhibit the following problems:

- Mechanical parts in the print head can wear out; but they last through several million characters.

- Worn ribbons and print head misalignment can cause print problems.

- A print head that is too far from the ribbon causes light print.

- A print head that is too close to the ribbon causes smearing, excess ribbon wear, and printed copy that is not smooth.

The paper transport mechanism in dot-matrix printers includes both pressure and tractor/pin feeders. If paper does not move through the printer, consider the following possibilities:

- Is the mechanism engaged?

- Are there broken gears in the drive train?

- Is the stepper motor burned out? This motor feeds paper and holds paper in place

 Turning the platen knob or pulling paper from a printer while it is online can destroy the stepper motor.

- Ink jet print heads, like dot-matrix print heads, problems. If this occurs, replace the ink jet cartridge.

- Is this ribbon cable defective? A defective ribbon cable can affect individual ink cylinders on an ink-jet printer or an individual print wire on a dot-matrix printer.

Laser Printer Problems

Identifying Your Printer Engine

A **printer engine** includes the drum and fusing mechanisms. Although many brands of laser printers are available on the market, many use engine rooms from a few manufacturers. Consequently, laser printer parts and supplies often are available from more than one manufacturer. By determining which engine your printer uses, you can improve your ability to find parts and supplies, and obtain more favorable prices.

Cleaning the Printer

Many common laser printer problems can be eliminated just by cleaning. Before calling for service on your printer, inspect the parts discussed in the following paragraphs for buildup of toner or dust, and clean them as necessary.

 Do not use a vacuum to clean laser printers, unless the vacuum is designed for laser service. The toner used in laser printers is very fine and is electrically conductive. Laser toner will ruin a standard vacuum. Toner vacuums have special fine filter cartridges to trap the toner and protect the vacuum motor. Many photocopier vacuums also have toner filter cartridges. Always turn off a printer before performing maintenance.

The Paper Path

If stains appear on the back of your paper, the paper path is dirty. The paper path includes the manual and automatic paper trays as well as flat surfaces inside the printer with which the paper comes into contact. You can clean the paper path with a laser toner vacuum or by wiping it with a damp cloth.

The rollers that pick up the paper from the paper tray must be cleaned occasionally or they are likely to harden with age. Use acetone or commercial rubber cleaners and a lint-free cloth to revitalize the rubber parts of these rollers. However, these cleaners are designed to soften rubber by dissolving the outer layer, and frequent use will damage rollers.

 Acetone is highly flammable. Exercise caution using and storing any flammable liquid.

The Filters

Most laser printers have one or more filters above the toner cartridge. Clogged filters can cause the printer to overheat, which can result in blurred text and graphics. Filters should be cleaned with a vacuum or cloth. Filters can get dirty if the printer is not adequately ventilated. Be sure walls or other objects do not crowd the printer.

The high voltage corona wires produce ozone while the laser is operating. An activated charcoal filter absorbs the ozone before it leaves the printer. Ozone can cause lung and eye irritations. If you smell a vinegar-like odor, it is time to replace the ozone filter.

The Corona and Transfer Wires

If your pages have white patches or vertical streaks, the corona wires and transfer wires in the printer cartridge might be dirty. Refer to your printer manual for the exact location of corona and transfer wires. They are so thin that you can have trouble seeing them. Some manufacturers supply a small cleaning tool for these wires, usually located inside the printer. Ensure that the tool itself is clean before using it. If not, you can use a vacuum to clean it. If the printer does not include a cleaning tool, wires can be cleaned with a Q-tip moistened with alcohol. Do not apply more pressure than necessary; these wires are fragile.

Hewlett Packard laser printers have a nylon string wrapped around the corona wire assembly. Be sure to clean the corona wire, not the nylon string.

The Separation Belt

Some laser printers have a three-inch plastic strip called the separation belt that guides the paper. Inspect it for smudges. Clean it with a cotton swab and water only. *Do not use chemical cleaners.* If the printer jams repeatedly, the belt could be broken. You can replace it yourself. In fact, a replacement belt often is stored in the printer. Refer to your user's manual for instructions about replacing the separation belt.

The Fuser Assembly

Recurring paper jams also indicate problems with the fuser rollers. The rollers are made of rubber so they can grab the paper. As they harden with age, they become less able to pick up the paper.

To prevent hardening, several times a year wipe the rollers with a Q-tip dipped in acetone. Be careful not to scratch the rollers. Also, be sure to leave the printer open while you clean the rollers; if acetone fumes linger in the printer, they can interfere with the electrical conductivity of the OPC drum.

 Do not use acetone on a hot fuser assembly! Remember acetone is extremely flammable.

The fuser assembly in many laser printers also includes a fuser wand, a piece of black plastic with a white felt strip that cleans toner buildup from the rollers. Refer to your user's manual to locate the fuser wand. The felt strip on the wand can become excessively dirty. Scrape the fuser wand gently with the edge of a paper clip. The fuser wand should be replaced when the cartridge is changed. Many toner cartridge kits include replacement fuser wands.

 The fuser assembly is very hot. Avoid contact with the fuser rollers unless the printer has been turned off for at least one hour.

If the rollers are badly scratched or the heat lamp is not working, you must replace the fuser assembly. Replacing the fuser rollers and heat lamp is not difficult. Refer to the user's manual or another resource for assistance.

Problems with paper

Often, using the wrong paper causes problems with laser printers. Paper that is too heavy causes misfeeds or paper jams, and paper that is too light or is embossed can cause multi-feeds. Embossed paper also can cause jams. Verify that you are using paper that meets the manufacturer's recommendations. Paper is described by the following characteristics:

- **Basis weight** is the weight of 500 sheets of 17" x 22.5" paper.

- **Caliper** is the thickness, in thousandths of an inch, or mils.

- **Finish** or **texture** is the surface smoothness, as measured in Sheffield, Gurley, Bekk, or Bendtsen units. Normal paper should be about 350 Sheffield units or about the texture of a new dollar bill. Rough paper wears out pick-up rollers and paper guides prematurely. Rough paper also degrades output quality. Paper that is too smooth results in misfeeds and poor toner adhesion, images from previous pages appearing on the current page (washout) and scattering of background toner.

- **Moisture content** is important. Paper exposed to humid air absorbs moisture like a dry sponge. Paper must pick up a strong static charge from the corona wire to attract toner from the OPC drum. Moisture dissipates static; therefore, moist paper will cause poor quality printing in a laser printer. Try opening and using a new ream of paper. If paper from a new ream prints well, moisture is probably the problem.

- **pH balance** affects the storage life of paper. pH balanced paper will last hundreds of years. Less expensive paper has an acid pH from the manufacturing process and will deteriorate over a few decades.

- **Grain curl** is the flatness, which you can check with a ruler. Too much grain curl causes paper jams and misfeeds.

- **Cut edge condition** refers to the edges of paper. You can inspect this with a magnifying glass. You should twist a new ream from the ends to separate sheets cleanly. This is known as breaking the ream. Fanning one end of a new ream of paper is less effective.

- **Fusing compatibility** is the ability of heated paper to absorb toner. Specialty papers are available that have superior ability to fuse with the toner.

Problems Related to the EP Process

Printed characters that smear easily indicate a fuser problem. The fuser usually is not hot enough to completely fuse the toner. Replacing the entire fuser assembly is usually the most cost effective alternative. Refurbished fuser assemblies are widely available.

Repeated problems of this type indicate scratches on the rollers or OPC drum. Replacing a combination toner cartridge fixes this, because the photosensitive drum, primary charging roller, and developing roller are contained in the cartridge. Inspect rollers and the OPC drum on printers that require separate replacement. Often you will see a scratch that matches the paper printing defect.

A self test allows you to check the transfer of toner to the drum, plus other factors. An absence of toner on the drum can indicate the following:

- Sealing tape was left on the cartridge.

- The toner cartridge is empty.

- The primary charging roller is not receiving power from contacts or high voltage power supply.

- The DC controller is malfunctioning.

- The laser beam path is obstructed.

- The shutter on the toner cartridge is stuck open or shut.

Use the Engine Test button on the printer, if available, to determine whether imaging problems reside in the print engine or in the formatter.

Quick Guide to Troubleshooting

The following table lists common problems you can encounter with your laser printer and offers possible solutions.

Problem	Try This
Paper jams	Inspect the rollers nearest the jam. Use acetone to soften rubber rollers that have hardened with age. Check the separation belt for possible replacement.
Print and graphics are darker on one side of the page.	Remove the cartridge and tilt it back and forth to redistribute the toner. Replace the toner cartridge or refill the toner reservoir. The developer also might need replacing if the previous steps do not fix the problem.
Smudges on printout when paper is manually fed	Feed several pages of heavy paper through the manual feed tray to clear dirt or spilled toner. It is normal for the first ten sheets of paper or so to have toner smudges following any service.
White patches or vertical streaks on page	Clean the corona and transfer wires. Clean or replace the fuser wand. Replace the fuser roller and heat lamp. Try paper from an unopened ream.
Stains on back of printed page	Clean the paper path with a damp cloth or run multiple sheets of paper through the printer until paper comes out clean. Gross stains can indicate a leaking toner cartridge.
Printer overheating or emitting a burning odor.	Clean the filter(s) with a toner vacuum or cloth and be sure the printer is adequately ventilated.

Setting Hardware Interrupts

It is very important that no two devices in a computer try to use the same interrupt. When installing a new expansion card, be sure to first determine which interrupts are already in use. Diagnostic software can detect interrupts, but only if the device that is assigned is operating. For instance, if a network interface card is using interrupt 10, diagnostic software would show IRQ 10 as available unless you load the network drives and log onto the network.

Computer devices commonly use some specific interrupts, but other interrupts are usually available. Unfortunately, expansion card manufacturers frequently use the same commonly available interrupt as their default setting. The first card installed can work well, but the second card installed will conflict with the first and cause both not to work.

IRQs 2 and 9 are called the **cascade interrupt**. Two 8-port interrupt controllers are cascaded to avoid using one 16-port controller. IRQs 2 and 9 are intended for internal controller use only. Some driver software has been specifically written to use IRQ 2. Under most circumstances, you should avoid using cascade interrupts for other devices.

You can refer to the following tables to resolve IRQ conflicts.

Interrupt Controller 1	
IRQ0	timer output
IRQ1	keyboard controller
IRQ2	secondary interrupt controller
IRQ3	serial port COM2
IRQ4	serial port COM1
IRQ5 .	available or used for parallel printer port 2 (LPT2) or the sound card
IRQ6	floppy disk controller
IRQ7	parallel printer port LPT1
Interrupt Controller 2	
IRQ8	real time clock
IRQ9	software redirect to IRQ2
IRQ10	available but may be used for a sound card
IRQ11	PCI Bus or SCSI Interface
IRQ12	PS/2 Mouse
IRQ13	math coprocessor
IRQ14	primary IDE (hard disk) controller
IRQ15	secondary IDE controller

Troubleshooting Tips

- Simplify the configuration. Remove all TSRs or clean boot the system. Boot the computer from a generic boot floppy to isolate operating system or software problems.

   Tip TSRs are programs that stay in memory after the user exits so that the program is immediately available via a hotkey. TSRs were used often in DOS for utilities that a user might want instant access to, such as a calculator. TSRs never were standardized and often conflicted with one another and other applications. The advent of Windows 3.1 reduced the need for TSRs.

- Remove expansion boards to isolate resource conflicts. You might have to remove all expansion boards except the video and hard drive controller to clear resource conflicts. Reinstall boards one at a time until the offending board is identified.

- When substituting hardware components, be sure the replacement part is reliable and operates properly. Hardware used for testing is handled frequently and is susceptible to electrostatic discharge (ESD) damage, jumpers falling off, or switches being changed accidentally. Always consider the possibility that the part being replaced and the replacement part are both bad. Test parts used for troubleshooting in a known good system to accurately verify their operation.

- Refer to diagnostic software, manufacturers' Internet sites, or help desks for assistance. In many cases, a five-minute conversation with a manufacturer's support technician can solve a known problem with their product.

LESSON 13: CUSTOMER SERVICE

After completing this lesson, you will be able to:

- understand the basic principles of customer service

- understand what customers want from you

- understand how to work with upset customers

- understand nonverbal communication

What is Customer Service?

Whether you work in a corporate computer support department or a commercial service organization, the individual computer user is your customer. When you assist customers, you are a representative of your company and your department. In that role, every judgment, action, and reaction you display reflects on the entire organization. To your customers, you *are* the company or the department.

Developing good customer relations and providing quality customer service is essential in today's business world, but too often technicians learn how to correct computer problems without showing any regard for the human behind the computer.

Components of Support Calls

Support calls, whether conducted in person or on the telephone, consist of the following essential components:

 If you are answering support calls on the telephone, remember the five components of a good phone voice:

Sound alert.
Sound pleasant.
Keep your tone conversational.
Speak distinctly by enunciating and articulating.
Speak with expression — vary the tone and the rate at which you speak.

◆ **Start with the greeting or the handshake.** This is your initial contact with a customer. How well the transaction progresses depends in large part on how you handle this initial contact. You should introduce yourself, ask the customer's name, ask for a customer or identification number if applicable, and ask what you can do to help.

- **Listen to the complaint**. Many people have poor listening habits, which can set the stage for bad encounter. Remember the five signs of a poor listener.:

  ‣ interrupting the speaker

  ‣ trying to have all the answers

  ‣ believing you always know more and have better judgment than the speaker

  ‣ overreacting

  ‣ only pretending to listen

- **Interview the caller**. Ask specific questions. You must ask the following three types of questions:

  ‣ **Background questions**. Explain briefly that you need background information so that you can answer the customer's questions completely. Customers can be quite frustrated and impatient. Don't reflect their impatience.

  ‣ **Probing questions**. Lead the conversation so that you can gather the information you need. Ask what happened, what the customer was doing when the problem first occurred, how long it has been happening, and other questions that can help you evaluate the situation.

▸ **Confirming questions**. Restate what the customer is telling you. In the midst of a problem is no time for miscommunication. Specifically ask, "So, what you are saying is..."

◆ **Closure**. You always hope that the closure to every call is to solve the problem, thank the customer, and complete the task. However, you cannot always resolve the situation completely. You may refer the customer to someone else, you may schedule a technical appointment, or you may escalate the procedure by passing the problem to a higher authority. If you cannot help the customer on the telephone or at the initial meeting, provide a specific timeframe in which they can expect the problem to be solved.

 A good rule of thumb when you must estimate when a task will be complete is to allow yourself 150% as much time as you believe the task will take. For example, if you think you can do the job in four business days, tell the customer six business days to be safe.

Communicating with Customers

Dealing with customers is difficult any time, but when you must communicate on the telephone or calm an angry customer, the challenge is even greater. Before this situation arises, take steps to understand why people become upset, what they expect from you, and various ways to communicate your message.

 If you communicate on the telephone, you have an even harder task. When we speak to someone in person, only 7% of our message's impact is in words, and 38% is in vocal quality. The largest percentage, 55%, is in nonverbal cues. When you work to solve someone's problems on the telephone, you cannot use those nonverbal cues. Everything comes from your words and the tone of your voice.

Why Do Customers Become Upset?

Customers are upset for many reasons. They might just be having a bad day, and nothing is going right. However, some you can avoid some reasons by understanding how to talk to customers before they get upset.

- Never promise what you cannot deliver. If you cannot do the job and must use an outside consultant, don't mislead the customer or try to make him or her believe you can take care of the situation immediately.

- Do not be rude or indifferent. One of the worst responses you can give is "Oh well." Show compassion and concern for the customer and try to accept what they say with a smile.

- Always present a pleasant attitude. Even if you are having a bad day, you cannot bring that to work with you. Put your best face forward for customers.

Guidelines for using the *on hold* option on the telephone:

- Ask permission first, and **wait** for an answer.

- Ask the customer how long they have been on hold and offer to speak with a supervisor about the problem if it has been too long.

- After keeping someone on hold for 30 seconds, check back to see if they want to continue holding.

- Never use "on hold" for more than three minutes without giving the customer an opportunity to leave a message and get a call back instead of waiting.

- Do not use the "on hold" feature if you can call the customer back instead.

- Always thank the customer for waiting and apologize when you finally get on the line.

- Listen. Really listening to what someone is telling you is difficult. You can use several techniques to improve your listening skills: take notes, ask questions, don't think about personal problems while you're listening, don't talk too much, don't interrupt, think like the customer and try to imagine the situation from the customer's point of view, don't jump to conclusions, listen for overtones in the customer's voice (read between the lines), concentrate on the customer and not those around you, and never patronize a customer. Though you must assume that the customer knows little about computers, do not talk down to the person or accuse the customer of doing something wrong.

- Never tell someone they have no right to be upset. You do not know their circumstances. What seems trivial to you can be of the utmost importance to a customer. Customers don't want to hear your opinions about their attitudes — only about their computers.

- Never give a smart or flip reply and never use obscenities; customers don't want to hear your locker room language.

- Do not point out that the situation could have been avoided if the customer had not made a mistake. In fact, you should not point out that a customer has made a mistake at all. If you discover that a situation occurred because a customer did something wrong, you must fix the system, then offer to give them some pointers about how to prevent this from happening in the future. That way, you can explain the correct way to do something without sounding accusatory.

- Never question the customer's integrity or honesty. A recent conversation at a help desk went like this:
  Customer: My PC speakers aren't working; when I plug them in they put out a really bad noise.
  Technician: Let me see the speakers.
  The *customer gives the speakers to the technician, who plugs them into a system and tests them, only to hear a horrible noise.*
  Technician: Well, I guess you really were telling the truth.

  This attitude makes the customer wary of the technician and likely to cause the customer to question any advice the technician gives.

- Do not argue with the customer. If the customer says the computer is turned on and plugged in, do not ask repeatedly whether they are sure the machine is plugged into the wall outlet. If the customer says he could not have caused the problem, do not argue the point.

What Can I Do?

When you are confronted with an upset customer, it is not always obvious what the person wants you to do about the situation. To determine and meet customers' expectations, consider the following general principles:

- Take customers seriously; do not attempt to downplay the situation and never tell a customer how much worse it could be.

- Treat customers with respect. Do not belittle a customer because they bought the cheapest model or a system that you would not recommend. Treat every customer as a unique human being, not a number.

- Take immediate action. Nothing is worse than telling someone you're too busy to estimate when you can fix something. If they bring a system or component into your shop, do not set the equipment aside while the customer is there. Leave it on the counter, talk to the customer, and tag the item while the customer watches.

- Offer compensation and/or restitution. Some customers want to be reimbursed for their troubles or want to avoid paying for equipment that doesn't work properly. Your organization should have a specific policy for this, but you also should consider special circumstances.

- Don't try to hide from the situation or your responsibility. Some customers want someone reprimanded or punished. This is particularly the case if the customer is returning a system that was supposedly fixed but still does not function. They may demand that you correct the situation. If you are the technician who worked on the equipment, and the customer asks to see your boss, do not hesitate to summon your supervisor.

- Resolve the problem so that it does not happen again. If you have learned anything relevant to the customer's troubles, be sure to point it out. If you have implemented new procedures or put new guidelines in place as a result of the customer's complaint, be sure to mention them.

- Listen to customers. Many people don't want you to really do anything; they only want to get the problem out in the open and have you listen to them.

Activity 5: Dealing with Upset Customers

Dealing with upset and demanding customers can be a stressful situation. If you think about this situation before it arises, you will be better prepared to respond. The following three situations are representative of the situations that occur frequently on help desks. Read each customer complaint and explain how you would respond.

1. I've been on hold for 20 minutes. What is taking so long?

   _____

   _____

   _____

   _____

   _____

2. You promised you would have my computer repaired two days ago. What is the problem? I want it fixed right now.

   _____

   _____

   _____

   _____

   _____

3. You've made my system worse. You're completely incompetent. Let me speak to your supervisor immediately.

   _____

   _____

   _____

   _____

   _____

Nonverbal Communication

Although good verbal skills are imperative on the telephone, you also may meet customers in person. If so, be aware that communication is more than words. Nonverbal communication makes up most of human communicating. The following list includes basic ideas you must remember as you communicate with others:

- **Facial expression**
  - Never roll your eyes.
  - Look at the customer.
  - Don't scowl.
  - Remain calm, concerned, and sincere.
- **Body posture**
  - Don't slouch; stand up confidently.
  - Don't crowd the customer; stand back and out of the customer's face.
- **Movement**
  - Don't move slowly when the customer expects action; you can finish that sandwich later.
- **Gestures (body language)**
  - Don't stand with your arms crossed.
  - Never use offensive gestures.
- **Smoking**
  - Don't smoke in sight of customers.

- **Touching**
  - Avoid touching customers.

- **Chewing gum/eating**
  - You cannot speak clearly with gum or food in your mouth. Do this outside the customer's presence.

- **Tone of Voice**
  - Don't sound annoyed, impatient, or condescending.
  - Sound competent and confident.

- **Sighing**
  - Don't sigh; it's a sign of impatience or boredom.

- **Cursing**
  - Never use foul language, even language that you consider mild, where customers can hear you; you could easily offend someone.

- **Physical appearance**
  - Pay particular attention to your personal appearance. Although technicians in general have no stringent dress code, you should strive to meet the following guidelines:
    - clean, combed, and well-kept hair
    - neat and moderate makeup, if any
    - conservative clothing that's pressed and well cared for
    - clean hands and nails
    - clean shave, if applicable
    - fresh breath

However you work with customers, you must take the time to cultivate relationships. Not only do good customers speak well of you to others, but hours go by much faster when you enjoy the experience.

Activity 6: Responding to Customer Questions

The following activity represents typical questions customers ask technicians. Following each question is an answer; however, these answers are not conducive to good customer relations. Explain in the lines below each one how you would answer the question and what is wrong with the indicated response.

1. *Question*: Why won't my system boot?
    Answer: Have you plugged in the machine?

    Why shouldn't you say this?

    _____

    _____

    How would you rephrase it?

    _____

    _____

2. *Question*: I can't make my printer work with my PC.
    Answer: Call the printer manufacturer; it's definitely a printer problem.

    Why shouldn't you say this?

    _____

    _____

    How would you rephrase it?

    _____

    _____

3. *Question*: I can't get my modem to connect.
    Answer: Check your manual. The troubleshooting procedures are in there.

    Why shouldn't you say this?

    _____

    _____

    How would you rephrase it?

    _____

    _____

4. *Question*: Can you tell me what the status is on my PC repair?
    Answer: The computer's down — check back tomorrow.

    Why shouldn't you say this?

    _____

    _____

    _____

    How would you rephrase it?

    _____

    _____

5. *Question*: Why hasn't my system been repaired yet? You promised me I could have it yesterday.
    Answer: Oh, you filled out the repair request incorrectly. Fill it out again and we'll look at it next week.

    Why shouldn't you say this?

    _____

    _____

    How would you rephrase it?

    _____

    _____

Sample Customer Service Report Form

Call Date:_____   **Priority Code: 1 2 3 4 5**

Customer Name:	**Customer #:**
Department/Division:	Phone: E-mail:

Equipment:		
Application:		Version:
Operating System:		Version:
Problem:		
Activity at time of first occurrence:		
Error messages:		
Actions taken prior to call:		
Prior history:		

Date reported:	Time reported:
Troubleshooting:	

Date promised:	Technician:
Action taken:	
Problem:	

Follow-up action:	Date completed:
Comments:	

Technician signature:
Customer signature:

Review

The four essential components of a customer support telephone call are as follows:

- the greeting or handshake

- listening to the complaint

- interviewing the caller

- closure

Customers become upset for a variety of reasons. If you follow a few simple guidelines, you can avoid some of those negative emotions.

Nonverbal communication accounts for more than 55% of getting the message across when we communicate face-to-face with another human being.

LESSON 14: RESOURCES

The following sections provide essential resources to help you locate the hardware, software, peripherals, and support you need. This lesson includes sections about the following resources:

- Vendor Resources
- Mail Order Resources
- Online Resources
- Technical Support Resources

The listings are in alphabetic order by company name, and the icons shown below indicate the major product or product lines of each company.

Cards and Boards

Digital Cameras

Input Devices

Modems

Monitors

Networks

Offsite Storage

PCs, Servers

Portable Computers

Power Supplies

Printers & Scanners

Processors, Chips, BIOS

Recovery Services

Software

Speakers

Storage Devices

Vendor Resources

The following pages contain the names, addresses, telephone numbers, Web addresses, and e-mail addresses of hardware and software manufacturers. The icons indicate the primary products that each company offers.

3COM (U.S. ROBOTICS)

8100 North McCormick Boulevard
Skokie, IL 60076-2920
847-982-5010
800-342-5877 (Sales)
800-550-7800 (Customer Service)
http://www.usr.com
Modems, Portable Computers, Networking cards

ACER AMERICA CORPORATION

2641 Orchard Parkway
San Jose, CA 95134
800-733-2237
408-432-6200
800-767-0334 (Sales)
800-637-7000 (Customer Service)
http://acer.com/aac
PCs

ACTIVE COMPONENTS

2802 N. Nevada Avenue, Suite 2
Colorado Springs, CO 80907
800-376-1581
719-477-1862
Fax: 719-477-1865
Computer Components

ADVANCED MICRO DEVICES, INC. (AMD)

408-732-2400
800-538-8450
http://www.amd.com
Microprocessor Chips

ADVANCED LOGIC RESEARCH, INC. (ALR)

9401 Jeronimo
Irvine, CA 92718
800-444-4ALR
714-581-6770
Fax: 714-581-9240
http://www.alr.com
PC Systems

AGFA: BAYER CORPORATION

AGFA Division
200 Balladvale Street
Willmington, MA 01887-1069
800-685-4271
201-440-2500
http://www.agfahome.com
Flatbed Scanners

AIMS LAB INC.

510-661-2525
http://www.aimslab.com
Video-to-Still Capture Cards

ALPS ELECTRIC

800-825-2566
408-432-6000
http://www.alps.com
Pointing Devices

ALTEC LANSING

P.O. Box 277
Milford, PA 18337-0277
800-ALTEC-88
http://www.altecmm.com
Speakers

ALTEK CORPORATION

301-572-2555
http://www.kurta.com
Pointing Devices

AMERICAN MEGATRENDS, INC. (AMI)

800-828-9264
770-246-8600
http://www.megatrends.com
BIOS Chips

AMERICAN POWER CONVERSION (APC)

132 Fairgrounds Road
West Kingston, RI 02892
800-800-4APC
http://www.apcc.com
Surge Suppressors, Uninterruptible Power Supplies

APEX DATA

A Division of SMART Modular Technologies
4305 Cushing Parkway
Fremont, CA 94538
510-623-1231
http://www.apexdata.com
MPEG-1 PC Card

APPLE COMPUTER INC.

One Infinite Loop
Cupertino, CA 95014-2084
800-776-2333
408-996-1010
800-776-2333 (Customer Service)
http://www.apple.com
Computers, Portable Computers, PowerPCs

APS TECHNOLOGIES

6131 Deramus
P.O. Box 4987
Kansas City, MO 64120-0087
800-418-6391
816-483-1600
Fax: 816-483-3077
E-mail to: sales@apstech.com
http://www.apstech.com
Storage, Backup, Universal Power Supplies, PC Accessories, Laptops

AST RESEARCH, INC.

16215 Alton Parkway
P.O. Box 57005
Irvine, CA 92618
800-876-4278
714-727-4141
http://www.ast.com
PCs, Workstations, Servers

ATRIEVA

888-287-4832
http://www.atrieva.com
Offsite Storage ($14.95/month unlimited space)
30-day Free Trial

AuraSound

2335 Alaska Avenue
El Segundo, CA 90245
800-909-AURA
http://www.aurasystems.com
Speakers

AVer Media

47923A Warm Springs Boulevard
Frèmont, CA 94539
510-770-9899
http://www.aver.com
MPEG Wizard External Encoder Box

Award Software International Inc.

415-237-6800
http://www.award.com
BIOS Chips

Banyan Systems, Inc.

120 Flanders Road
P.O. Box 5013
Westboro, MA 01581
508-898-1000
800-222-6926 (800-2-BANYAN)
Fax: 508-898-1755
Fax Back: 800-932-9226
http://www.banyan.com
Networking, Intranet, and Messaging Products

BEST POWER

P.O. Box 280
Necedah, WI 54646
800-356-5794
http://www.bestpower.com
Uninterruptible Power Supplies

BOCA RESEARCH INC.

1377 Clint Moore Road
Boca Raton, FL 33487
561-997-6227
561-241-8088
http://www.bocaresearch.com
Modems

BOSE CORPORATION

The Mountain
Framingham, MA 01701
800-444-BOSE
http://www.bose.com
Speakers

BREEZECOM, INC.

2195 Faraday Avenue, Suite A
Carlsbad, CA 92008
760-431-9880
Fax: 760-431-2595
http://www.breezecom.com
Wireless Networking Products

BROTHER INTERNATIONAL

200 Cottontail Lane
Somerset, NJ 08875-6714
908-356-8880
http://www.brother.com
Printers

CABLETRON SYSTEMS

35 Industrial Way
Rochester, NY 03867
603-332-9400
http://www.cabletron.com
Wiring Closet Switches

CALCOMP TECHNOLOGIES, INC.

800-458-5888
714-821-2689
http://www.calcomp.com
Pointing Devices, Accessories, Keyboards

CAMBRIDGE SOUNDWORKS

311 Needham Street
Newton, MA 02164
800-FOR-HIFI
http://www.hifi.com
Speakers

CANON COMPUTER SYSTEMS, INC.

2995 Redhill Avenue
Costa Mesa, CA 92626
One Cannon Plaza
Lake Success, NY 11042-9979
800-848-4123
714-438-3000
http://www.canon.com
http://www.ccsi.canon.com
Printers, Digital Cameras

CARDINAL TECHNOLOGIES

717-293-3124
http://www.cardtech.com
Modems

CASIO

800-962-2746
201-361-5400
http://www.casio.com
http://www.casiohpc.com (Handheld PCs)
Digital Cameras, Handheld PCs

C-CUBE MICROSYSTEMS, INC.

1778 McCarthy Boulevard
Milpitas, CA 95035
408-944-6300
http://www.c-cube.com
Video Chips

CH Products

970 Park Center Drive
Vista, CA 92083
760-598-2518
800-624-5804 (Sales and Customer Service)
http://www.chproducts.com
Input Devices

CheckPoint Software Technologies

Redwood, CA
800-429-4391
http://www.checkpoint.com
Firewalls

CIC

800-888-8242
415-802-7888
http://www.cic.com
Pointing Devices

Cisco Systems, Inc.

170 West Tasman Drive
San Jose, CA 95134-1706
800-553-NETS (6387)
408-526-4000
Fax: 408-526-4100
800-859-2726 (Sales)
800-GO-CISCO (Small/Medium Business Products Division)
http://www.cisco.com
Networking, Internet, Intranet Products

CMD TECHNOLOGIES

800-426-3832
714-454-0800
http://www.cmd.com
PCI to USB Adapter

CNF, INC.

15345 Calle Enrique
Morgan Hill, CA 95037
800-8CNF-INC
http://www.cnfinc.com
PC Card Reader

COMPAQ

20555 State Highway 249
Houston, TX 77070-2698
800-345-1518
281-514-0484
800-888-5925 (Sales and Customer Service)
http://www.compaq.com
PCs, Notebooks, Laptops, Workstations, Servers

CONNECTED CORPORATION

http://www.connected.com/products/prodfram.htm
Offsite Backup Services (*Connected Online Backup 2.5*)

CoStar Corporation

800-426-7827
203-661-9700
http://www.costar.com
Pointing Devices

Creative Labs, Inc.

1901 McCarthy Boulevard
Milpitas, CA 95035
800-998-1000
408-428-6600
http://www.creativelabs.com
http://www.soundblaster.com
Sound Cards and Sound Peripherals
CD-ROM and DVD Drives

Crucial Technology

A Division of Micron Electronics
8455 W. Emerald
Boise, ID 83704
888-363-2565
208-363-5500
Fax: 208-363-5501
E-mail to: crucial.sales@micron.com
http://www.crucial.com
Memory

CTX International, Inc.

20470 Walnut Drive
Walnut, CA 91789
800-888-2120
http://www.ctxintl.com
Monitors

CyberLAN, Inc.

565 Brea Canyon Road, Unit B
Walnut, CA 91789
909-444-9669
http://www.cyberlanwireless.com
Wireless Networks

CyberMedia, Inc.

3000 Ocean Park Boulevard
Santa Monica, CA 90405
310-581-4700
http://www.cybermedia.com
Security and Privacy software (*Guard Dog Deluxe*), Crash and
Recovery Software (*First Aid*)

Cyrix Corporation

800-777-9988
http://www.cyrix.com
Microprocessor Chips

DATA FELLOWS

408-938-6700
http://www.datafellows.com
AntiVirus Software (*F-PROT Professional, F-Secure Anti-Virus*)

DATA TRANSLATION, INC.

100 Locke Drive
Marlboro, MA 01752
800-249-1000
508-481-3700
http://www.b-way.com
Video Capture Cards

DAYNA COMMUNICATIONS, INC.

A Division of Intel
849 West Levoy Drive
Salt Lake City, UT 84123
800-44-DAYNA
http://www.dayna.com
Network Equipment

DELL COMPUTERS

One Dell Way
Roundrock, TX 78682
800-854-6245
800-624-9897 (Customer Service)
800-289-1180 (Sales)
http://www.dell.com/buydell
PCs, Portable Computers, Workstations, Servers

DELTEC

2727 Kurtz Street
San Diego, CA 92110
800-845-2658
http://www.deltecpower.com
Uninterruptible Power Supplies

DIAMOND MULTIMEDIA SYSTEMS

2880 Junction Avenue
San Jose, CA 95134-1922
800-468-5846
408-325-7000
http://www.diamondmm.com
Video Cards, Sound Cards, Graphics/Video Boards

DOLBY LABORATORIES

100 Potrero Avenue
San Francisco, CA 94103
415-558-0200
http://www.dolby.com
Sound Cards

DR. SOLOMON

888-DRSOLOMON
781-273-7400
http://www.drsolomon.com
AntiVirus Software (*Dr. Solomon's Anti-Virus*)

DRAGON SYSTEMS, INC.

800-825-5897
617-965-5200
http://www.naturalspeech.com
Voice Recognition Software

DRIVESAVERS

800-440-1904
415-382-2000
http://www.drivesavers.com
Data Recovery Services

EASTERN RESEARCH, INC.

225 Executive Drive
Moorestown, NJ 08057
800-377-4374
Fax: 609-273-1847
http://www.erinc.com
Networking, Wireless, Internet, and WAN products

EASTMAN KODAK COMPANY

800-235-6325
http://www.kodak.com
Digital Cameras

ELO TOUCHSYSTEMS

800-ELO-TOUCH
http://www.elotouch.com
Touch Screens

EPSON AMERICA, INC.

20770 Madrona Avenue
P.O. Box 2842
Torrance, CA 90509-2842
800-533-3731(Customer Service)
800-463-7766
310-782-0770
http://www.epson.com
Printers, Scanners

EXIDE ELECTRONICS

8609 Six Forks Road
Raleigh, NC 27615
800-554-3448
http://www.exide.com
Uninterruptible Power Supplies

FAST MULTIMEDIA

800-248-3278
http://www.fastmultimedia.com
Video Capture Cards

FTG Data Systems

800-962-3900
714-995-3900
http://www.ftgdata.com
Pointing Devices

Gateway 2000 Inc.

610 Gateway Drive
P.O. Box 2000
North Sioux City, SD 57049-2000
800-846-2000
605-232-2000
http://www.gateway.com
http://www.gw2k.com
PCs, Portable Computers, Workstations, Servers

Genicom Corporation (Texas Instruments)

One Solutions Way
Waynesboro, VT 22980
540-949-1000
800-436-4266
Printers

Gyration Inc.

800-316-5432
408-255-3016
http://www.gyration.com
Pointing Devices

HAYES MICROCOMPUTER PRODUCTS, INC.

5953 Peachtree Industrial Boulevard
Norcross, GA 30092
770-840-9200
770-441-1617 (Customer Service)
800-377-4377
http://www.hayes.com
Modems

HELIX SOFTWARE COMPANY

800-451-0551
718-392-3100
http://www.helixsoftware.com
Problem Solving Software (*Nuts & Bolts*)

HEWLETT-PACKARD COMPANY

P.O. Box 58059
Santa Clara, CA 95051-8059
3000 Hanover Street
Palo Alto, CA 94304
800-752-0900
800-637-7740 (Sales)
650-857-1501
408-246-4300
http://www.hp.com
Printers, Scanners, PCs, Handheld PCs, Workstations, Servers

HITACHI DATA SYSTEMS

750 Central Expressway
Santa Clara, CA 95050
408-970-1000
800-227-1930 (Sales)
http://www.hdshq.com
CD-ROM Drives

HITACHI DIGITAL GRAPHICS, INC.

408-735-0577
http://www.hitachidigital.com
Pointing Devices

HiVAL

1300 E. Wakeham Avenue
Santa Ana, CA 92705
714-953-3000
http://www.hival.com
Drives

IBM

New Orchard Road
Armonk, NY 10504
800-426-3333
800-426-2968 (Sales)
800-742-2493 (Software Division)
http://www.pcco.ibm.com
www.ibm.com
PCs, Portable Computers, Workstations, Servers
AntiVirus Software (*IBM AntiVirus*)

IDEAL SCANNERS AND SYSTEMS, INC.

11810 Parklawn Drive
Rockville, MD 20852
301-468-0123
Fax: 301-230-0813
http://www.ideal.com
Large Document Scanners, Document Acquisition and Distribution

INFO PERIPHERALS

580 Division Street
Campbell, CA 95008
408-538-2500
http://www.infoconnection.com
Scanners

INTEL CORPORATION

800-538-3373
503-264-7354
http://www.intel.com
Microprocessor Chips

INTERLINK ELECTRONICS

800-340-1331
805-484-8855
http://www.interlinkelec.com
Pointing Devices

IOMEGA CORPORATION

800-MY-STUFF
801-778-1000
Removable Backup Drives (*Jaz* and *Zip Drives*)

JAZZ

1355 Darius Court
City of Industry, CA 91745
800-291-8999
http://www.jazzspeakers.com
Speakers

KDS USA, INC.

12300 Edison Way
Garden Grove, CA 92641
800-237-9988
http://www.keytronic.com
Monitors

KENSINGTON TECHNOLOGIES GROUP

2855 Campus Drive
San Mateo, CA 94403
800-535-4242
415-572-2700
http://www.kensington.com
Pointing Devices, Input Devices

KEYTRONICS INC.

P.O. Box 209
Endicott, NY 13761-0209
607-754-5405
800-262-6006
http://www.keytronics.com
Input Devices

KINGSTON TECHNOLOGY CORPORATION

http://www.kingston.com
800-588-5428
714-435-2600
Memory

KOSS

4129 N. Port Washington Avenue
Milwaukee, WI 53212
800-USA-KOSS
http://www.koss.com
Speakers

LABTEC ENTERPRISES, INC.

3801 109th Avenue, Suite J
Vancouver, WA 98682
360-896-2000
http://www.labtec.com
Speakers

LEXMARK INTERNATIONAL INC.

740 New Circle Road NW
Lexington, KY 40550
606-232-2220
800-438-2468
http://www.lexmark.com
Printers

LIEBERT CORPORATION

1050 Dearborn Drive
Columbus, OH 43229
800-877-9222
http://www.liebert.com
Uninterruptible Power Supplies

LOGITECH INC.

29959 Ahern Avenue
Union City, CA 94587
800-231-7717
510-795-8500
http://www.logitech.com
Pointing Devices, Input Devices

LOTUS DEVELOPMENT CORPORATION

55 Cambridge Parkway
Cambridge, MA 02142
800-343-5414
617-577-8500
http://www.lotus.com
Software

LUCENT TECHNOLOGIES

600 Mountain Avenue
Murray Hill, NJ 07974
888-584-6366
http://www.lucent.com
Wireless Networks

MAG INNOVISION

2801 S. Yale Street
Santa Ana, CA 92704
714-751-2008
800-827-3998 (Sales)
http://www.maginnovision.com
Monitors

MATROX GRAPHICS, INC.

1055 St. Regis Blvd.
Dorval, Quebec H9P 2T4
Canada
514-969-6320
800-361-1408 (Sales and Customer Service)
514-685-2638
http://www.matrox.com
Graphics/Video Boards

MAXTOR CORPORATION

510 Cottonwood Drive
Milpitas, CA 95035
800-2-MAXTOR
http://www.maxtor.com
Drives

MEMORY PLUS, INC.

46 East Main Street
Westboro, MA 01581
800-388-7587
508-366-2240
Fax: 508-366-7344
http://www.memoryplus.com
Memory, CPUs, Hard Drives, Controllers

MGE UPS SYSTEMS, INC.

1660 Scenic Avenue
Costa Mesa, CA 92626
714-557-1636
http://www.mgeups.com
Uninterruptible Power Supplies

MICRON ELECTRONICS, INC.

900 E. Karcher Avenue
Nampa, ID 83687
800-423-5891
888-634-8799
800-438-3343 (Sales)
208-898-3434
Fax: 208-893-7393
http://www.micronpc.com
PCs, Portable Computers, Servers, Workstations, Memory

MICROSOFT CORPORATION

One Microsoft Way
Redmond, WA 98052
800-426-9400 (Sales and Customer Service)
425-882-8080
http://www.microsoft.com
Software, Keyboards, Pointing Devices, Network Software

MICROTEK LAB, INC.

3715 Doolittle Drive
Redondo Beach, CA 90278
800-654-4160
http://www.microtekusa.com
Scanners

MICROTOUCH SYSTEMS, INC.

800-642-7686
508-659-9000
http://www.microtouch.com
Pointing Devices

MIDILAND

440 S. Lone Hill Avenue
San Dimas, CA 91773
909-592-1168
http://www.midiland.com
Speakers

MITSUMI ELECTRONICS CORPORATION

800-648-7864
http://www.mitsumi.com
Disk Drives

MOBILITY ELECTRONICS

800-311-3279
602-596-0061
http://www.mobilityelectronics.com
Portable Computers

MOTHERBOARD EXPRESS COMPANY

333 W. State Road
Island Lake, IL 60042
800-560-1195
http://www.motherboardx.com
Motherboards

MOTOROLA

50 East Commerce Drive
Schaumburg, IL 60173
847-576-5000
http://www.mot.com
Modems

MOTOROLA WORLDWIDE

Data Solutions Division
1301 E. Algonquin Road
Schaumburg, IL 60196
800-247-2346
800-894-7353 (PC Cards)
http://www.mot.com
Wireless Networks, PC Cards, Microprocessor Chips

MOUSE SYSTEMS CORPORATION

510-656-1117
http://www.mousesystems.com
Pointing Devices

MUSTEK

1702 McGraw Avenue
Irvine, CA 92614
714-247-1300
http://www.mustek.com
Scanners

NEC ELECTRONICS, INC.

888-632-8698
http://www.nec.com
PCs, Servers, Portable Computers

NEC Technologies, Inc.

1414 Massachusetts Avenue
Boxborough, MA 01719
800-632-4636 (MultiSync Display Division)
800-692-4636
888-306-4636 (Sales)
978-264-8000
http://www.nec.com
Monitors

NetBack

http://www.netback.com/backsvc.html
Online Backup Services

Netscape Communications Corporation

501 E. Middlefield Road
Mountain View, CA 94043
415-254-1900
415-937-3777 (Sales)
415-937-2555 (Customer Service)
E-mail to: client@netscape.com
http://home.netscape.com
Internet and Intranet Software

Netwave Technologies, Inc.

6663 Owens Drive
Pleasanton, CA 94588
510-737-1616
http://www.netwave-wireless.com
Wireless Networks

Network Associates (McAfee)

2710 Walsh Avenue
Santa Clara, CA 95051
800-332-9966
408-988-3832
http://www.mcafee.com
AntiVirus Software (*VirusScan*), Crash & Recovery Software (*PC Medic*)

http://www.networkassociate.com
Offsite Storage ($10/month, 30 MB storage space)

New Castle International

603-431-6170
http://www.newcastleintl.com
AntiVirus Software (*inVircible*)

New Media Corporation

800-227-3748
714-453-0100
http://www.newmediacorp.com
PC Cards

Novell

1555 North Technology Way
Orem, UT 84097
801-222-6000
888-321-4272 (Sales and Customer Service)
http://www.novell.com
Networking Hardware and Software

NUMBER NINE VISUAL TECHNOLOGY CORPORATION

18 Hartwell Avenue
Lexington, MA 02173
800-GET-NINE
800-438-6463
617-674-0009
http://www.nine.com
Graphics Cards/Video Boards

OKIDATA

532 Fellowship Road
Mount Laurel, NJ 08054
800-654-3282 (Sales)
609-235-2600
E-mail to: comments@okidata.com
http://www.okidata.com
Printers

ONTRACK DATA INTERNATIONAL

800-872-2599
612-937-5161
http://www.ontrack.com
Data Recovery Services

OPTIUPS CORPORATION

1050 W. Central Avenue, Suite E
Brea, CA 92821
888-OPTI-UPS
http://www.opti-ups.com
Uninterruptible Power Supplies

OPTIQUEST

20480 Business Parkway
Walnut, CA 91789
800-888-8583
http://www.viewsonic.com
Monitors

THE OTHER 90% TECHNOLOGIES INC.

888-329-9899
http://www.other90.com
Pointing Devices

PACKARD BELL

One Packard Bell Way
Sacramento, CA 95828-0903
888-211-4159 (Customer Service)
800-733-5858 (Sales)
916-388-0101
http://www.packardbell.com
PCs

PANASONIC COMMUNICATIONS AND SYSTEMS CO.

Matsushita Electric Corporation
Two Panasonic Way
Secaucus, NJ 07094
201-348-7000
http://www.panasonic.com
CD-ROM and DVD Drives, Speakers

PANASONIC COMPUTER PERIPHERAL COMPANY

1707 N. Randall Road, Suite #1-D3
Elgin, IL 60123
847-468-4600
800-742-8086 (Sales)
http://www.panasonic.com
Printers

PCL COMPUTER, INC.

636 Lincoln Highway
Fairless Hills, PA 19030
215-736-0846
PC Cases

PCMCIA

408-433-2273
http://www.pc-card.com
PC Cards

PHILIPS SEMICONDUCTORS

P.O. Box 3409
Sunnyvale, CA 94088-3409
800-234-7381
http://www.semiconductors.philips.com
TriMedia TM1000 Video Processor

PHOENIX TECHNOLOGIES, INC.

408-570-1000
http://www.phoenixtech.com
BIOS Chips

PINNACLE COMPUTER RESOURCES

450 Fenton Lane #901B
West Chicago, IL 60185
888-278-7271
630-293-3400
Fax: 630-293-3495
Components, Memory

PLAY INC.

916-851-0800
http://www.play.com
Video-to-Still Capture Cards

PLEXTOR

4255 Burton Drive
Santa Clara, CA 95054
408-980-1838
800-886-3935 (Sales)
E-mail to: info@plextor.com
http://www.plextor.com
CD-ROM Drives

POLAROID CORPORATION

565 Technology Square
Cambridge, MA 02139
800-816-2611
http://www.polaroid.com
Scanners and Digital Cameras

POWERQUEST

800-720-0399
http://www.powerquest.com
Disk Maintenance Software (*PartitionMagic, DriveImage, DriveCopy*)

PROTEON, INC.

Nine Technology Drive
Westborough, MA 01581-1799
800-545-7464
508-898-2800
http://www.proteon.com
Networking Products

PROXIM INC.

295 N. Bernardo Avenue
Mountain View, CA 94043
415-960-1630
http://www.proxim.com
Wireless Networks

QUANTUM CORPORATION

500 McCarthy Boulevard
Milpitas, CA 95035
408-894-4000
800-624-5545 (Sales)
800-345-3377
http://www.quantum.com
Hard Drives

QUARTERDECK CORPORATION

800-683-6696
813-523-9700
http://www.quarterdeck.com
Problem Solving Software (*REALHELP*)

RADIOLAN, INC.

455 DeGuigne Drive
Sunnyvale, CA 94086
408-524-2600
http://www.radiolan.com
Wireless Networks

REYNOLDS DATA RECOVER SERVICE

800-223-7483
303-776-7110
http://www.sni.net/reynolds
Data Recovery Services

RICOH CORPORATION

800-955-3453
408-432-8800
702-352-1600 (Digital camera division)
http://www.ricoh.com
CD-ROM Drives
Digital Cameras

SAFEGUARD INTERACTIVE

412-415-5200
http://www.sgii.com
Offsite Storage ($9.95/month Unlimited Storage)

SAMSUNG

105 Challenger Road
Ridgefield Park, NJ 07660
201-229-4000
800-726-7864
http://www.samsung.com
Monitors

SC&T INTERNATIONAL, INC.

15695 North 83rd Way
Scottsdale, AZ 85260
602-368-9490
http://www.platinumsound.com
Speakers

SCEPTRE TECHNOLOGIES, INC.

16800 E. Gale Avenue
City of Industry, CA 91745
888-580-5588
http://www.sceptretech.com
Monitors

SEAGATE TECHNOLOGY INC.

P.O. Box 66360
Scotts Valley, CA 95067-0360
408-438-6550
408-439-2924 (Sales)
800-468-3472
http://www.seagate.com
Hard Drives

SECURE COMPUTING

800-692-5625
http://www.securecomputing.com
Firewalls and Encryption Software

SHARP ELECTRONICS

800-237-4277
201-529-8200
http://www.sharp-usa.com
Portable Computers, Handheld PCs

SIGMA DESIGNS

46501 Landings Parkway
Fremont, CA 94538
800-845-8086
http://www.realmagic.com
DVD/MPEG-2 Playback Card

SIMPLE TECHNOLOGY

800-464-6753
714-476-1180
http://www.simpletech.com
PC Cards

SL WABER

520 Fellowship Road, Suite 306-C
Mount Laurel, NJ 08054
800-634-3485
http://www.slwaber.com
Uninterruptible Power Supplies

SONY ELECTRONICS

3308 Zanker Road
Cypress, CA 95134
408-432-1600
800-222-7669 (Sales)
800-282-2848 (Customer Service)
800-352-SONY
http://www.sony.com
DVD-ROM Drives; Monitors

SSI

11836 Clark Street
Arcadia, CA 91006-6000
800-845-4774
Speakers

SYMANTEC CORPORATION

10201 Torre Avenue
Cupertino, CA 95014
800-441-7234
541-334-6054
408-253-9600
http://www.symantec.com
AntiVirus Software (*Norton AntiVirus*), Crash & Recovery Software
(*Crash Guard*)
Diagnostic Software (*Norton Utilities*)

SYMBOL TECHNOLOGIES, INC.

One Symbol Plaza
Holtsville, NY 11742-1300
800-354-3556
http://www.symbol.com
Wireless Networks

SYQUEST TECHNOLOGY

800-245-2278
510-226-4000
Removable Backup Drives

TATUNG

2850 El Presidio Street
Long Beach, CA 90810
800-827-2850
310-637-2105
http://www.tatung.com
Monitors

TEAC AMERICA, INC.

213-726-0303
http://www.teac.com
Disk Drives

TENFOUR

14595 Avion Parkway, Suite 500
Chantilly, VA 20151
800-837-0046
Fax: 703-263-2120
http://www.tenfour.com
Connectivity Solutions for LANs

THUNDERBYTE

800-667-8228
613-930-4444
http://www.thunderbyte.com
AntiVirus Software (*ThunderBTYE Anti-Virus Utilities*)

TOSHIBA

9740 Irvine Boulevard
Irvine, CA 92713
800-334-3445
888-598-7802 (Sales)
800-959-4100 (Accessories)
800-999-4273
714-583-3000 (Customer Service)
http://www.toshiba.com
Portable Computers, PCs

TOTAL RECALL

800-743-0594
719-380-1616
http://www.recallusa.com
Data Recovery Services

TOUCHSTONE SOFTWARE CORPORATION

714-969-7746
http://www.checkit.com
AntiVirus Software (*Pc-cillinll*)

TRAVELING SOFTWARE INC.

18702 North Creek Parkway, Suite 102
Bothell, WA 98011
425-483-8088
800-343-8080
http://www.travsoft.com
Remote Access Software

TRI STATE COMPUTER

650 Sixth Avenue
New York, NY 10011
800-433-5199
212-633-2530
Fax: 212-633-7718
PCs and Peripherals

TRIPP LITE POWER PROTECTION

500 N. Orleans
Chicago, IL 60610
312-755-5400
312-755-8741
Fax: 312-644-6505
Fax Back Information: 312-755-5420
E-mail to: info@tripplite.com
http://www.tripplite.com
Uninterruptible Power Supplies

TURTLE BEACH SYSTEMS

5 Odell Plaza
Yonkers, NY 10701
800-233-9377
http://www.tbeach.com
Sound Cards

TYAN COMPUTER CORPORATION

1753 South Main Street
Milpitas, CA 95035
408-956-8000
http://www.tyan.com
Motherboards

UBISOFT ENTERTAINMENT

625 Third Street
San Francisco, CA 94107
800-UBI-SOFT
http://www.ubisoft.com
Sound Cards

UMAX TECHNOLOGIES, INC.

3561 Gateway Boulevard
Fremont, CA 94538
800-562-0311
510-651-4000
http://www.umax.com
Scanners

VIDEOLOGIC, INC.

1001 Bayhill Drive
San Bruno, CA 94066
415-875-0606
http://www.videologic.com
GrafixStar 400 mm Accelerator and MPEG Star Cards

VIDEONICS

1370 Dell Avenue
Campbell, CA 95008
408-866-8300
http://www.videonics.com
Python Frame Grabber

VISIONEER

510-608-0300
http://www.visioneer.com
Scanners

WACOM TECHNOLOGY CORPORATION

800-922-6613
360-896-9833
http://www.wacom.com
Pointing Devices

WATERGATE SOFTWARE, INC.

510-596-2080
http://www.ws.com
Problem Solving Software (*PC-Doctor for Windows*)

WESTERN DIGITAL CORPORATION

8105 Irvine Center Drive
Irvine, CA 92718
714-932-5000
800-832-4778 (Sales and Customer Service)
http://www.wdc.com
Hard Drives

WINBOOK CORPORATION

1160 Steelwood Road
Columbus, OH 43212
800-468-7502
614-481-7466
800-254-7806 (Sales)
http://www.winbook.com
PCs

XING TECHNOLOGY CORPORATION

810 Fiero Lane
San Luis Obispo, CA 93401
800-294-6448
http://www.xingtech.com
XingMPEG Encoder

YAMAHA

6600 Orangethorpe Avenue
Buena Park, CA 90620
714-522-9011
http://www.yamaha.com
Speakers

Mail Order Sources

This section lists the major mail order sources of computers,
peripherals, cabling, accessories, and software. Unless specifically
indicated, these resources sell a variety of products, including
hardware, PC systems, peripherals, and software. Prices are usually
lower if you can purchase through a third-party vendor, such as these,
rather than directly from the manufacturer.

BIG CITY EXPRESS

96 Hobart Street
Hackensack, NY 07601
888-232-CITY

CAD WAREHOUSE

8515 Freeway Drive, Suite B3
Macedonia, OH 44087
800-487-0485
216-487-0590

CompUSA DIRECT

34 St. Martin Drive
Marlborough, MA 01752-3021
800-438-4312
972-528-7000

COMPUTABILITY

P.O. Box 17882
Milwaukee, WI 53217
800-554-2186
Fax: 800-554-9981
Fax: 414-357-7814
http://www.computability.com

COMPUTER DISCOUNT WAREHOUSE

1020 E. Lake Cook Road
Buffalo Grove, IL 60089
800-895-4239
800-681-4239
http://www.cdw.com

COMPUWORLD, INC.

CompuWorld Building
Corbin Drive
Cleveland, OH 44126
216-332-0000
800-6666CW1
Fax: 216-332-0FAX
http://www.Compu-World.com

DIRT CHEAP DRIVES

3716 Timber Drive
Dickinson, TX 77539
800-473-0962
281-534-4140
Fax: 281-534-6452
http://www.dirtcheapdrives.com

DIGITAL VIDEO DIRECT

3001 Clark Street
Champaign, IL 61821
217-355-2785
888-383-4732
Fax: 217-356-4312
http://www.dvdirect.com
E-mail to: solutions@dvdirect.com

EXEL COMPUTER

401 Park Avenue, South
New York, NY 10016
800-486-EXEL

HARMONY

1801 Flatbush Avenue
Brooklyn, NY 11210
718-692-3232
718-692-2828
800-898-7275
http://www.shopharmony.com

INSIGHT COMPUTERS

6820 S. Hart Avenue
Tempe, AZ 85283
800-927-3171
602-902-1176

INTERNET PARADISE (DIVISION OF PROGRAMMER'S PARADISE)

1163 Shrewsbury Avenue
Shrewsbury, NJ 07702-4321
800-344-2495
732-389-9229
800-441-1511 (Corporate Accounts)
Fax: 732-389-9227
http://www.pparadise.com
Internet/Intranet Software Only

J & R COMPUTER WORLD

59-50 Queens Midtown Expressway
Maspeth, Queens, NY 11378
800-221-8180
Fax: 800-232-4432

L. A. TRADE

22825 Lockness Avenue
Torrance, CA 90501
800-433-3726
310-539-0019
Fax: 310-539-5844
E-mail to: sales@LATrade.win.net
http://www.4LATrade.com

MICROWAREHOUSE

1702 oak Street
Lakewood, NJ 08701
908-370-0518
800-304-1934
Fax: 732-905-5245
http://www.warehouse.com

MIDWEST MICRO

6910 US Route 36 East
Fletcher, OH 45326
800-413-9785

PC MALL

2645 Maricopa Street
Torrance, CA 90503-5144
800-532-2292
http://www.pcmall.com

PC ZONE

707 S. Grady Way
Renton, WA 98055-3233
800-258-2088

PINNACLE COMPUTER RESOURCES

450 Fenton Lane #901B
West Chicago, IL 60185
888-278-7271
630-293-3495
Fax: 630-293-2495
http://www.pcrlink.com

POWER UP! (A TIGERDIRECT COMPANY)

8700 W. Flagler Street, 4th Floor
Miami, FL 33174-2428
800-335-4055
800-888-4437
305-228-5200
Fax: 800-782-1435
http://www.tigerdirect.com

PRINTER CONNECTION

P.O. Box 927240
San Diego, CA 92192
800-479-6090

PROGRAMMER'S PARADISE

1163 Shrewsbury Avenue
Shrewsbury, NJ 07702-4321
800-445-7899
800-344-2495
Fax: 732-389-9227
http://www.pparadise.com
Software Only

PROGRAMMER'S SUPERSHOP™

1163 Shrewsbury Avenue
Shrewsbury, NJ 07702-4321
800-421-8006
732-389-8950
Fax: 732-389-0010
732-389-9229
800-421-2510 (Corporate Accounts)
http://www.supershops.com
Software Only

TIGERDIRECT

800-888-4437
305-228-5200
Fax: 800-782-1435
http://www.tigerdirect.com

TriState Computer

650 Sixth Avenue
New York, NY 10011
800-433-5199
212-633-2290

Web Resources

This section lists some of the many resources on the Web for finding general information. This is just a small sampling of what is available online.

ANCHORDESK

http://www.zdnet.com/anchordesk
Updated industry information, reviews, and shareware

BOOT MAGAZINE

http://www.bootnet.com
Hardware reviews, industry news, shareware, and links

BYTE

http://www.byte.com
Hardware and software benchmarks, reviews, technical information, downloads, JobNet, and a 4-year online article archive from the print magazine

CNET

http://www.cnet.com
Shareware, reviews, information on new technology

COMPUTER DIGEST

http://www.gy.com/computer
Links to hardware manufacturers, software developers, storage media manufacturers, and wholesale/retail resources

COMPUTER SHOPPER

http://www.cshopper.com
Hardware and software reviews, information sources, articles on the latest technology

COMPUTERWORLD

http://www.computerworld.com
Industry news, career/job information, computer-related books

DRIVER ZONE

http://www.driverzone.com
Drivers for hundreds of computers and peripherals, plus links to the technical departments for the original equipment

NETWORK

http://www.networkmagazine.com
Archive of all articles in the print magazine since 1995, links to relevant sites, glossary of terms, tutorials about network-related topics

PC COMPUTING

http://www.pccomputing.com
General industry information, reviews of new technology

PC MAGAZINE

http://www.pcmag.com
Utilities, articles, hardware reviews

PC TODAY

http://www.pctoday.com
Reviews, articles, extensive tips and troubleshooting section

PC Week

http://www.pcweek.com
Industry news, downloads, reviews

PC World

http://www.pcworld.com
Industry news and reviews
(Note: this site does not work well with Microsoft Internet Explorer 4.0)

Window95.com

http://window95.com
Downloadable software, tips and tricks, links to other sites

Windows Magazine

http://www.winmag.com
Reviews, articles, shareware, online forums, and discussion groups

Technical Support Resources

This section lists the Web addresses, technical and customer support telephone numbers, and the e-mail addresses of major manufacturers. Online resources often are quite thorough, and you may want to check online before calling the technical support department.

3COM (U.S. ROBOTICS)

http://www.3com.com
Technical Support: 847-982-5151
Customer Service: 800-550-7800
E-mail to: support@usr.com

ACER AMERICA CORPORATION

http://www.acer.com/aac
Technical Support: 800-733-2237

ADOBE SYSTEMS, INC.

http://www.adobe.com
BBS: 206-623-6984
Faxback: 206-628-5737
E-mail to: techdocs@adobe.com
800-833-6687

APPLE COMPUTER INC.

http://www.apple.com
Technical Support: 800-767-2775
Customer Service: 800-776-2333

AST RESEARCH INC.

http://www.ast.com
Technical Support: 800-876-4278
Customer Service: 800-876-4278
E-mail to: web.support@ast.com

BOCA RESEARCH INC.

http://www.bocaresearch.com
Technical Support: 561-241-8088
Customer Service: 561-241-8088
E-mail to: support@bocaresearch.com

BROTHER INTERNATIONAL

http://www.brother.com
Technical Support: 800-276-7746
Technical Support in California: 714-859-9700, ext. 329

CANON

http://www.ccsi.canon.com
Technical Support: 800-423-2366
Customer Service: 800-423-2366

CHEYENNE SOFTWARE, INC.

http://www.cheyenne.com
BBS: 516-465-3900
Faxback: 516-465-5979
Fax Tech Questions to: 516-465-5115
Network Technical Support: 800-243-9832
Desktop Technical Support: 516-465-6600
Customer Service: 800-243-9462

CISCO SYSTEMS, INC.

http://www.cisco.com
http://www.cisco.com/public/support (Online Help Files)
800-553-2447
408-526-7209
E-mail to: tac@cisco.com

COMPAQ COMPUTER CORPORATION

http://www.compaq.com
Technical Support: 800-652-6672
Customer Service: 800-888-5925
E-mail to: support@compaq.com

DELL COMPUTER CORPORATION

http://www.dell.com
Technical Support: 888-560-8324
Customer Service: 800-624-9897
E-mail to: support@us.dell.com

DIAMOND MULTIMEDIA SYSTEMS

http://www.diamondmm.com
Technical Support: 408-325-7100
Customer Service: 800-468-5846
E-mail to: techsup@diamondmm.com

EPSON AMERICA INC.

http://www.epson.com
Technical Support: 800-922-8911
Customer Service: 800-533-3731

GATEWAY 2000 INC.

http://www.gateway.com
Technical Support: 800-846-2301
Customer Service: 800-846-2000

GENICOM CORPORATION (TEXAS INSTRUMENTS)

Genicom Customer Service: 540-949-1031
Texas Instruments: 888-774-6843
Customer Service: 800-436-4266

HAYES MICROCOMPUTER PRODUCTS

http://www.hayes.com
Technical Support: 770-441-1617
Customer Service: 771-441-1617
E-mail to: techsupport@hayes.com

HEWLETT-PACKARD

http://www.hp.com
Technical Support: 800-858-8867
Customer Service: 800-752-0900

IBM CORPORATION

http://www.ibm.com
Technical Support: 800-772-2227
Customer Service: 800-772-2227
E-mail to: askibm@info.ibm.com

IOMEGA

http://www.iomega.com
BBS: 801-778-4400
Technical Support: 801-629-7610
Customer Service: 801-629-7630

KENSINGTON TECHNOLOGIES

http://www.kensington.com
Technical Support: 415-572-2700

KEYTRONICS INC.

http://www.keytronics.com
Technical Support: 800-262-6006

LEXMARK INTERNATIONAL INC.

http://www.lexmark.com
Technical Support: 606-232-3000

LOGITECH INC.

http://www.logitech.com
Technical Support: 702-269-3457
Customer Service: 800-231-7717

MAG INNOVISION

http://www.maginnovision.com
Technical Support: 800-827-3998
Customer Service: 800-827-3998

MATROX GRAPHICS INC.

http://www.matrox.com
Technical Support: 514-685-0270
Technical Support: 514-685-2552
Customer Service: 800-361-1408

MICRON ELECTRONICS INC.

http://www.micronpc.com
Technical Support: 800-349-6972
Customer Service: 800-438-3343
E-mail to: techsupport.meic@micron.com

MICROSOFT CORPORATION

http://www.microsoft.com
Faxback: 800-936-4200
Recorded tips: 800-936-4200
Technical Support Directory: 800-426-9400
Customer Service: 206-882-8080
Windows 95 Support: 425-635-7000

MOTOROLA

http://www.mot.com
Technical Support: 800-934-4721

NEC TECHNOLOGIES INC.

http://www.nec.com
CD-ROM Technical Support: 800-632-4667
Monitor Technical Support: 800-632-4662
Notebook Technical Support: 800-632-4525
PowerMate Technical Support: 800-632-4565
Printer Technical Support: 800-632-4650
Ready Line Technical Support: 800-632-4554
E-mail to: tech-support@nectech.com

NETSCAPE COMMUNICATIONS CORPORATION

http://www.netscape.com
Technical Support: 800-639-0939
Fax back: 800-639-0939
Customer Service: 415-937-2555

PACKARD BELL

http://www.packardbell.com
Technical Support: 800-244-0049
Customer Service: 888-211-4159
E-mail to: support@packardbell.com

PANASONIC COMPUTER PERIPHERAL COMPANY

http://www.panasonic.com
Technical Support: 800-222-0584
Technical Support for Computers: 800-222-0584

PLEXTOR

http://www.plextor.com
Technical Support: 408-980-1838
Customer Service: 408-980-1838
E-mail to: info@plextor.com

PROTEON, INC.

http://www.proteon.com
http://www.proteon.com/contact/index.html (Technical Support Documents)
508-898-3100 (Internetworking Equipment)
Fax: 508-366-9146 (Internetworking Equipment)
508-898-2800 (PC/LAN Equipment)
Fax: 508-366-7930 (PC/LAN Equipment)

QUANTUM CORPORATION

http://www.quantum.com
Technical Support: 800-826-8022
Customer Service: 800-345-3377

QUARTERDECK CORPORATION

http://www.quarterdeck.com
Technical Support: 573-875-0530
Utilities Products Support: 573-875-0932
Customer Service: 310-309-3700

SAMSUNG

http://www.samsung.com
Technical Support: 800-726-7864
Customer Service: 800-726-7864

SEAGATE TECHNOLOGY INC.

http://www.seagate.com
Technical Support: 800-732-4283
Customer Service: 800-468-3472

SONY

http://www.sony.com
Technical Support: 800-326-9551
Customer Service: 800-282-2848

SYMANTEC CORPORATION

http://www.symantec.com
BBS: 541-484-6669
Fax back: 541-465-8555
Customer Service: 800-441-7234

TATUNG

http://www.tatung.com
Technical Support: 310-637-2105

WESTERN DIGITAL CORPORATION

http://www.wdc.com
Technical Support: 800-832-4778
Customer Service: 800-832-4778

WINBOOK CORPORATION

http://www.winbook.com
Technical Support: 800-468-122

GLOSSARY

absolute-position devices

Pointing devices that move in relation to a fixed, or absolute, point.

Accelerated Graphics Port (AGP)

Provides a pathway, or bus, from the CPU to the main system RAM. AGP offers a 66 MHz, 64-bit pathway that increases to 133 MHz per second for transfers and burst mode provides up to 528 MB per second transfers.

American Standard Code for Information Interchange (ASCII)

ASCII is a code that assigns an 8-bit combination of 1s and 0s to 256 characters, including letters, numbers, punctuation marks, and symbols. ASCII was developed in 1968 and is built into all PCs.

ammeter

A device that measures current flow through a circuit, in amps.

asynchronous transmission

An operation that occurs independently of a timer or clock.

basic input output system (BIOS)

A set of instructions stored in a PC's read-only memory that starts each time a system starts.

basis weight

The weight of 500 sheets of 17x22.5" paper.

baud rate

Number of signal changes per second that occurs with the transmission of data using a modem.

blackout

A complete loss of power. See also *sag, brownout,* and *undervoltage.*

bootable diskette

See *system disk.*

bridge

A device that provides a communication pathway between two or more network segments, forming one logical network. There are two types of bridges: local and remote bridges. See also *local bridge* and *remote bridge.*

brouter

A device that combines the technologies of a bridge and a router.

brownout

A prolonged period of undervoltage. See also *undervoltage, brownout,* and *sag.*

bus

A system of pathways that connect the CPU to devices attached to the motherboard.

bus topology

A LAN topology in which a single cable is used to connect all workstations in a daisy-chain fashion. All workstations share a single cable for transmission purposes.

byte

A byte is a unique set of eight bits that represent a specific letter, number, or other character.

cache

A memory area in which frequently used data is copied for quick access. When the processor refers to a memory address, the cache checks for the address first, before searching regular memory.

caliper

thickness in thousandths of an inch, or mils.

carrier sense

A network process by which devices monitor the cable to see whether data are being transmitted.

cathode ray tube (CRT)

The basic component of both a television set and a microcomputer monitor, composed of a large vacuum tube with a flat screen at one end and an electron gun at the other. The electron gun fires electrons at phosphors on the surface of the screen, illuminating them.

central processing unit (CPU)

The Central Processing Unit, or CPU, is the central control or "brain" of the computer that interprets and carries out every instruction.

charge coupled device (CCD)

A device in which individual semiconductors cause the output of one component to provide the input for the next. Charge-coupled devices are used in scanners.

client/server network

A local area network (LAN) with two distinct components: a "front-end" client and a "back-end" server. Each client is a stand-alone, fully functioning PC. The server is a PC, minicomputer, or mainframe that makes programs, files, data, and resources available to clients and provides administrative and security for the network.

clock speed

The number of clock cycles per second at which the CPU is capable of working. Clock speed is measured in MHz. There is an internal clock speed and an external clock speed.

cluster

The smallest portion of a disk that can store file data. A cluster may contain from 4 to 64 sectors. A file must comprise at least one cluster, regardless of how small the file is.

coaxial cable

Type of LAN cable that consists of a single copper wire surrounded by insulation, wrapped with braided copper to shield it from outside electrical signals and internal signal radiation.

collision detection

A network process of determining that multiple stations have transmitted data at the same time, blocking communication.

complimentary metal-oxide semiconductor (CMOS)

Contains hardware data for a system, including the type of hard drive, amount of memory, disk drive information, and the location of the operating system that the BIOS uses during startup.

complex instruction set computing (CISC)

A processor designed so that each instruction can perform several low-level operations, such as memory access, arithmetic operations, or address calculations.

controller

Translates electronic (digital) data from the computer into magnetic signals understood by drives.

conventional memory

The first 640 KB of memory available on a PC.

cross-linked file

Two different files in the FAT that claim the same cluster number as part of their file. Cross-linked files indicate a serious problem in the system. See also *file allocation table (FAT)*.

cut edge condition

The condition of the edge of the paper.

cyclic redundancy checking (CRC)

A process for error-checking data transmissions, using a mathematical calculation. The sending and receiving devices perform the calculation; if the results match, the transmission is determined to be error-free.

cylinder

The same track on different disk surfaces.

data bus

See *data path size.*

data path size

The amount of data the bus can transfer at one time. Also called the *data bus.*

data transfer rate

The speed, in bits and megabits per second (bps or mbps) at which a circuit or communication line transfers data between the hard disk or the CD-ROM and the CPU.

debouncing

A method used to filter keyboard noise. A key must be pressed for at least two scans before the signal is sent to the CPU.

density

How tightly data is packed on a disk.

direct memory access

Memory that can be directly accessed without going through the processor. Often referred to as a DMA channel.

disk operating system (DOS)

The part of the computer that manages the IPOS cycle and interfaces between the PC and the user. See *input-process-output-storage.*

disk striping

A technique for spreading data over multiple disk drives to increase operating speed.

dot-matrix printer

Type of printer that forms characters by placing a series of dots on the page.

dots per inch (dpi)

A measure of printer resolution using the number of dots a dot-matrix printer can print per linear inch.

drive array

A collection of multiple independent drives in one chassis or multiple drives that act as one logical drive.

dual in-line package (DIP)

The casing housing microprocessor chips. The electronic circuits are etched on a silicon wafer, then enclosed in a rectangular plastic or ceramic case. All of this is connected to pins lining both sides of the case. The pins then fit onto the circuit board.

electro-magnetic interference (EMI)

Interference caused by devices using magnetic energy, such as a computer monitor.

electrophotographic (EP) process

A process that uses a laser beam to create and transfer an image to a photosensitive drum. Toner is applied to the paper and the image is then transferred and fused to the paper.

electrostatic discharge (ESD)

Static electricity transmitted from an outside source to the circuit. The human hand is the most common outside source.

enhanced standard device interface (ESDI)

A device that allows computers and disks to communicate at high speeds — up to about 10 or 20 megabits per second.

expanded memory

Memory that operates by swapping information in and out of conventional memory using a 64-KB page frame in the upper memory areas. See also *conventional memory, upper memory areas*, and *page frame*.

Extended Industry Standard Architecture (EISA)

A standard developed to complete with IBM's MCA bus to support both 16- and 32-bit interface cards. See also *micro-channel architecture (MCA)*.

extended memory

System memory beyond 1 MB.

extended partition

The inactive partition of a hard drive.

file allocation table (FAT)

A list containing information about where files are stored in the disk's data area.

finish

See *texture*.

firewire

A high-speed serial bus designed for high-speed devices such as hard drives, CD-R drives, and full motion video editing.

format

To prepare a disk to store data. Formatting includes physical (low level) and logical (high level).

fragmentation

A situation in which parts of a single file are scattered to various locations on the disk. A disk with fragmentation is said to be fragmented. See also *fragmented*.

fragmented

The state of a disk drive when many files occupy non-contiguous sectors. Data on a fragmented disk is accessed more slowly.

frequency modulation

An early encoding technique, or method of storing data on disks, allowing storage bit-by-bit or character-by-character. An improved method is modified frequency modulation (MFM).

full-duplex line

A line that transmits and receives data in both directions at the same time.

fusing compatibility

The ability of the heated paper to absorb toner.

gateway

A device that serves as a translator to connect two incompatible networks.

grain curl

The flatness of a piece of paper.

graphics mode

A type of monitor that will use pixels to display images.

half-duplex line

A line that transmits or receives data, but not both at the same time.

Hamming code

A family of error-correction codes named for R. W. Hamming of Bell Labs.

high level format

See *logical format.*

high memory

The first 64 KB of memory above the 1 MB conventional memory. Older computers relied on third-party software to manage that high memory area, but Microsoft later include a file, called HIMEM.SYS, in the operating system to handle that memory.

hot swap

A feature that lets you connect equipment to the computer while it is powered on, instead of needing to turn the computer off to connect equipment.

hub

A device that joins network lines at a central location.

impact printer

Type of printer with print heads that strike a ribbon, leaving an imprint on the page.

Industry Standard Architecture (ISA)

The standard that allows you to add components by plugging cards into expansion slots.

inkjet printer

Type of printer that sprays ink on the page through a print . nozzle.

input-process-output-storage (IPOS)

The computer processing cycle that turns raw data into useable information.

integrated circuits (ICs)

A unit that contains microscopic digital switches known as transistors. These transistors process all information you enter into a computer. The central processing unit is the most important but only one of many integrated circuits on the motherboard. See also *central processing unit* and *motherboard*.

integrated drive electronics (IDE)

A form of disk-drive interface in which the controller electronics are on the drive itself, removing the need for an adapter card.

interface

A card or plug connecting hardware, such as a hard drive, to the computer so information can be shared between components.

interlaced

A type of monitor that requires two complete scans to redraw the screen. Every odd row is redrawn on the first scan, and every even row is redrawn in the second scan.

interleaved memory

Memory that organizes addresses in RAM so that adjacent locations are stored in different rows of chips. In this way, after accessing one byte, the processor can access additional bytes without having to wait an entire memory cycle before accessing the next byte.

laser printer

Type of printer that uses an electrophotographic process to transfer toner.

letter-quality printer

A type of printer that prints at a level that is crisp and dark enough for business use.

local area network (LAN)

A group of computers in a relatively small area connected so that all system can interact. A LAN usually includes PCs and shared resources such as printers and servers.

local bridge

Bridges used to connect LANs, usually within the same building. See also *bridge* and *remote bridge*.

logical format

A process performed with operating system software to establish the file structure. Also called *high level formatting*.

loopback

To transmit signals in the opposite direction as the result of a break in a ring network.

lost cluster

A disk storage unit designated by the operating system as being in use, but not representing any portion of a chain of stored file segments.

low level format

See *physical format*.

master boot record (MBR)

A section of the floppy or hard drive that contains a master partition table and master boot code the computer needs each time it starts.

master drive

In a master/slave drive arrangement, the master drive controls the secondary, or slave, drive. See also *slave drive*.

media surface

Both sides of a disk platter.

megahertz (MHz)

A measure of frequency. One megahertz equals 1 million cycles per second.

Micro Channel Architecture (MCA)

The standard used in most IBM PS/2 computers. There are 16- and 32-bit versions of the MCA bus.

modem

Derived from MOdulator DEModulator, a modem converts digital signals from a computer into analog signals that are sent over phone lines. On the other end, another modem converts the analog signals back into digital signals.

modified frequency modulation (MFM)

An encoding technique, or method of storing data on disks. MFM is less efficient than run length limited (RLL).

monitor

See *cathode ray tube (CRT)*.

motherboard

The main PC circuit board that contains all the chips needed to make the system work. The motherboard is also called the *system board* or *planar board*.

multimedia personal computer (MPC)

A personal computer with a minimum of an 80486SX CPU, 4 MB of RAM, 3.5" high density floppy disk drive, and 160 MB hard drive.

multimeter

A multi-purpose test instrument used by electronics technicians to test the operation of circuits, identify wiring faults, and check for the proper wiring of electrical outlets.

multiple access

A networking term meaning that any station can use the cable.

Multiple Access Unit (MAU)

The hub in a Token Ring network, to which workstations connect. The ring is contained within the hub. Also known as a Multi-Station Access Unit (MSAU).

network operating system (NOS)

The hardware and software comprising a local area network.

non-impact printer

Type of printer that uses a process or special print head that transfers toner or ink to the page.

noninterlaced

A type of monitor that redraws all rows of the screen on each scan to eliminate flicker and produce a better quality picture.

nonvolatile memory

Memory that remains intact even in the event of a power loss or if you remove the memory from the circuit board.

null modem cable

A device used to physically connect two microcomputers via serial ports for data transmission purposes, thus eliminating the need for a modem.

ohm

A unit of electrical resistance between two points that produces a current of one ampere. One megohm is equal to one million ohms.

ohmmeter

A device that measures circuit resistance by injecting a DC voltage and measuring changes to the test voltage.

overvoltage

A higher than normal voltage, usually caused by lightning strikes, power grid switching, cycling pump or compressor motors, photocopiers, laser printers, and other office equipment devices.

page frame

A section of memory set aside to shuttle the data between the memory areas. The page frame is actually virtual memory. See also *virtual memory*.

paper weight

The weight in pounds of 500 sheets of 17 x 22.5" paper.

parallel cable

Cables that transmit eight data bits at a time with each bit being transmitted on a separate line.

parity

The equivalence of two groups. In error checking, parity ensures that the number of 1s and 0s is exactly the same in two separate groups.

partition

Logical areas into which a hard disk is divided. Partitioning allows the creation of smaller logical drives of different sizes.

partition table

A listing of the way in which the hard disk is divided into logical drives.

PC card

See *Personal Computer Memory Card Industry Association (PCMCIA) card bus*.

peer-to-peer network

A network of at least two PCs directly connected to each other. Every system is a peer, or equal, and there is no server.

Peripheral Component Interconnect (PCI) local bus

The bus designed by Intel for the Pentium processor. This bus supports 32- and 64-bit cards and is compatible with ISA and EISA slots. See also *Industry Standard Architecture (ISA)* and *Extended Industry Standard Architecture (EISA)*.

Personal Computer Memory Card Industry Association (PCMCIA) card bus

A standard created primarily for laptops, palmtops, and other portable computers in a 16- and 32-bit interface. Also known as a PC Card.

physical format

Normally performed at the factory, an operation that lays out magnetic track and sector boundaries on the disk surface.

Pin Grid Array (PGA)

A square casing first used with the 80286 processor that had pins protruding from the bottom rather than from the edges as was the case in the DIP. This was the preferred packaging for chips with a large number of pins. See also *dual in-line processor (DIP)*.

pixels

Picture elements, the smallest element that hardware and software can use to create characters or graphics.

planar board

See *motherboard*.

platter

One of the individual plates, coated with material in which data is magnetically recorded, that make up a hard drive.

pointer

Indicates where the next cluster is for a file that spans multiple clusters.

power on self test (POST)

A series of tests a computer undergoes upon powering on.

primary partition

The active partition, usually identified as drive C, that boots the system.

radio frequency interference (RFI)

Noise in an integrated circuit caused by interference from a radio or television.

Random Access Memory (RAM)

Memory that provides temporary, or volatile, read and write storage of data. See also *read-only memory, volatile,* and *nonvolatile.*

Read-only Memory (ROM)

Memory that is widely used to store software and data because it is nonvolatile. See also *nonvolatile, volatile,* and *random access memory.*

read/write head

A device that moves across a platter to access data on a hard disk.

reduced instruction set computing (RISC)

A processor designed to rapidly execute a sequence of simple instructions rather than a large variety of complex instructions.

redundant array of inexpensive disks (RAID)

A security method involving a disk array. RAID has seven levels that provide different degrees of reliability and fault tolerance.

refresh rate

How often the entire screen is redrawn to maintain a constant image.

relative-position devices

Pointing devices that move in relation to the last position.

remote bridge

A bridge that has a port for analog or digital telecommunication links to other locations. See also *bridge* and *local bridge.*

repeater

A device inserted along a circuit to amplify an analog signal or regenerate a digital signal.

ribbon cable

Used to connect floppy disk drives to their controllers.

ring topology

A LAN topology where a closed loop of communication is managed by a central hub.

rotational latency

The time required for the data to rotate under the read/write head.

router

A device that learns the location of the network components, routes information to them, and chooses the best way to send the information from place to place.

run length limited (RLL)

An encoding technique that stores bit patterns as codes, rather than individual bits or characters. RLL is more efficient than modified frequency modulation (MFM).

sags

A short period of lowered voltage. See also *undervoltage, brownout,* and *blackout.*

sector

Pie-shaped slice of disk track.

seek time

The time required for the read/write head to move from one track (or cylinder) to another.

serial cable

Type of cable that transmits only one bit of data at a time.

servo

An electromechanical device that uses feedback to stop and start functions, such as the moving of an access arm on a disk.

shielded twisted pair (STP)

A type of LAN cable that has foil wrapping around each pair of wires and around the entire bundle, with a woven copper braid wrapped around the entire assembly.

slave drive

In a master/slave drive arrangement, the slave drive does not have a drive controller. Instead, it is controlled by the master drive. See also *master drive.*

small computer system interface (SCSI)

A standard high-speed interface defined by The American National Standards Institute (ANSI). SCSI is an independent data bus that functions without the direct intervention of the computer processor. See also *bus.*

software cache

A program that uses available RAM to store frequently used data.

spike

A short overvoltage, measured in billionths (nanoseconds) or millionths (microseconds) of a second. See also *overvoltage*.

star topology

A LAN topology using a hub as a central controller; each workstation is connected to the hub by a cable.

startup disk

Contains the programs necessary to boot a system, such as IO.SYS, MSDOS.SYS, and COMMAND.COM. Also called a *startup diskette* or a *bootable diskette*.

surge

An overvoltage that lasts longer than a spike, measured in thousandths of a second (milliseconds). See also *spike* and *overvoltage*.

synchronous transmission

A method of data transmission in which data is sent in blocks with regular time intervals between transmissions.

system board

See *motherboard*.

system diskette

See *startup disk*.

terminal emulation

Uses one computer to simulate the type of terminal required to gain access to another computer.

termination

Installing electrical resistors, or terminators, at each end of a bus so that commands and data can travel uninterrupted along the bus. Correct termination prevents signal reflection at the ends of the bus that can result in data corruption. You have to be particularly careful with SCSI termination. See also *small computer system interface (SCSI)*.

text mode

A type of monitor that displays symbols in arrangements of 80 columns and 25 rows.

texture

Surface smoothness as measured in Sheffield, Gurley, Bekk, or Bendtsen units.

throughput

The speed of processing data, usually measured in bit rates.

token

A special packet of information that controls access to the media transferred between systems.

Token Ring network

A network protocol that involves the use of a token. The token is passed between workstations; a workstation can transmit data only if it has the token. See *token*.

topology

The actual configuration of the connections between LAN devices.

track

Concentric circular areas on a disk where the data are stored.

transistor-transistor logic (TTL)

A type of semiconductor less prone to ESD damage than CMOS circuitry.

twisted-pair cable

A type of cable made up of two insulated strands, twisted together. One acts as the ground; the other carries the signal.

undervoltage

Voltage that is lower than normal, commonly caused by overloaded circuits.

uninterrruptable power supply (UPS)

A backup power supply that connects the PC directly to a battery.

Universal Serial Bus (USB)

A new bus that is tended to replace all other external interface ports. Users will be able to connect up to 127 peripherals to one PC using USB.

unshielded twisted pair (UTP)

A type of cabling that contains twisted pairs of wires without additional shielding.

upper memory blocks (UMB)

The 384 KB area of memory located immediately above conventional memory and is intended for system use.

Vendors Electronics Standards Association (VESA) local bus

A video bus that included a proprietary high-speed slot that could operate at the same speed as the processor. VESA was replaced by the PCI bus. See also *Peripheral Component Interconnect (PCI) bus.*

virtual memory

Memory that appears larger to an application than it is, usually by using part of the hard disk as temporary memory storage.

volatile memory

Memory that disappears when the system is powered off, or if there is a power loss of at least 4 milliseconds.

voltmeter

A device that measures alternating current or direct current.

Volt-Ohm Meter (VOM)

A multimeter capable of reading volts, ohms, and amperes.

word size

The amount of data the microprocessor processes internally at one time.

Index